ABERDEEN CURIOSITIES

ACKNOWLEDGEMENTS

A number of people helped to open up this wonderland. My thanks go particularly to the Local History Department of Aberdeen Central Library, and to many others who gave me their support.

Robert Smith
Aberdeen, 1997

ABERDEEN
CURIOSITIES

ROBERT SMITH

JOHN DONALD PUBLISHERS
EDINBURGH

This revised edition published in 2002 by
John Donald Publishers
an imprint of Birlinn Ltd
West Newington House
10 Newington Road
Edinburgh
EH9 1QS

www.birlinn.co.uk

First published in 1997 by
John Donald Publishers Ltd, Edinburgh

ISBN 0 85976 569 5

British Library Cataloguing-in-Publication Data
A catalogue record for this book is available
from the British Library

Typesetting and origination by Brinnoven, Livingston
Printed and bound by Antony Rowe Ltd, Chippenham

CONTENTS

1
CURIOUSER AND CURIOUSER

This is a book about curiosities. When John Aubrey, the English author and antiquary, wrote about curiosities back in the 17th century, he said, 'These curiosities would be quite forgot, did not such idle fellows as I am put them down.' It is more than likely that the curiosities in this book would also have been 'quite forgot' if they hadn't been 'put down'.

Nowadays, although people have the usual inquisitive interest in odd events, they never make the fuss that was seen two hundred years ago when it was announced that 'two great Curiosities' were coming to Aberdeen. The whole town got excited about it. In fact, the 'Curiosities' caused such a stir that even 'the principal gentry of this city' went out of their way to see them.

So what were these two great Curiosities? Well, one was 'a common Spaniel Dog'. The other was 'a little horse'. They appeared at one of the shows that regularly set up their tents and caravans on any vacant piece of ground in the city. The dog was said to give 'extraordinary performances in calculation' and the little horse showed 'amazing sagacity in answering most questions demanded of him'.

The local newspaper noted that the proprietor took 'no more than one penny for each person's admission'.

Even more popular was Mr Pidcock's famous lion, which was 'the terror and admiration of thousands of visitors'. It had been in Mr Pidcock's possession for ten years and when it died it was sadly missed. During its last illness the lion was attended by seven physicians.

The ground behind the Facade in Union Street, now part of St Nicholas churchyard, was where menageries and panoramas set themselves up. They could stay there as long as they wanted and one wild beast show stayed so long that it went bankrupt. Everything was auctioned and many townsfolk became the owners of monkeys, parrots and cockatoos. In 1816, Polito's Menagerie, the biggest that had ever been seen in the north, took a site there.

Panoramas were among the great 'Curiosities' early in the 19th century. In 1802 you could see, for a sixpence, a 'panorama with motion' of the Battle of the Nile, shown in Provost Jopp's Close in Broad Street. In 1821 it was bigger and better – a panorama of the 'Bombardment at Algiers' in Auchintoul's New Hall in Union Street. It was accompanied by a military band at each of its five daily performances.

Aberdeen had its own Madame Tussaud's two centuries ago. There were different exhibitions of waxworks in which 'the likenesses of some of the most distinguished characters of the last and present age are preserved with great accuracy and effect'. Record crowds turned out when Napoleon's imperial coronation robes and mantles were on view at Mr Fyfe's house in Exchange Court.

The pantomimes of today seem tame affairs compared with a performance that at one time boasted a Female Curiosity. This is what the *Aberdeen Journal* had to say about it:

> The grand and interesting spectacle of 'Blue Beard' or 'Female Curiosity' was brought out at the Aberdeen Theatre on Monday Last. Few pieces give more latitude for the display of scenery, machinery, and dresses. The whole performance was received with rapturous applause. The Elephant was the first ever introduced in Scotland upon the stage.

Sporting wagers were all the rage in those days. A young man from Woodside took on a wager for a bottle of whisky that he could pick up 100 stones, at a distance of one yard from each other, in a space of one hour. He did it with twelve minutes and thirty seconds to spare.

Another bet was made by a tradesman from Angus who offered – 'for a trifling wager' – to eat at one meal 28 ounces of pork fat, fried with butter, along with 5 biscuits, and to wash it down he would drink 4 gills of gin, 4 gills of milk and a Scotch pint of water. There is nothing to show whether or not he won his bet.

This new, extended edition of *Aberdeen Curiosities* tells you about more odd people and strange happenings . . . about the Battle of Castlehill and the man who fell down a chimney pot, about how the authorities played musical chairs with Royal statues, about husbands who were made to 'Ride the Stang' and about the eerie mystery of the gateposts. That and much more. As Alice would have said, it gets 'curiouser and curiouser'.

2
Scarty's Monument

Scarty's Momument stands near Fittie at the end of the North Pier – a tall, red-brick obelisk looking down on ships entering and leaving Aberdeen Harbour. It is an ugly structure, about 15 feet in height, and there is nothing on it to indicate who or what it commemorates.

So who was Scarty? His real name was William Smith (Scarty was his nick-name) and he was one of two pilots who kept watch at the North Pier in the middle of the 19th century. The other pilot was James Morrice, who was known as 'Pengie'.

Scarty's Monument.

Piddly Guyan.

Some anonymous scribe wrote a poem suggesting that there *should* be a plaque telling you about the Monument. It went like this:

I'll tell you o' a Monument
Erected in this Toon.
It stands doon by the Fisher Squares
An' built wi' bricks a' roon.
Oh it would look much better
If they'd gi 'en 't a coat o' paint
And stuck a brass plate on the front
O Scarty's Monument.

The poem mentions a local character who had the unkind nickname of 'Piddly' Guyan. He must have lived in the middle of the 19th century, for a sketch of him appeared in William Skene's *East Neuk Chronicles*, which featured Aberdeen worthies between 1840 and 1860. The Scarty poem wonders what 'peer auld Piddly Guyan' would have thought if he had seen 'this great erection'. He would open his eyes in surprise,

And the pair o' them would squint
Tae see a brass plate on the front
O' Scarty's Monument.

The colourful ventilator at the corner of Holburn Street and Justice Mill Lane.

Sadly, there is nothing heroic or romantic about Scarty's Monument. The only thing it celebrates is the pong that comes from a sewer which empties itself into the navigation channel. It is, in fact, a ventilator shaft for the sewer.

Nearly two miles away, at the junction of Holburn Street and Justice Mill Lane, is another 'Monument' which puzzles passers-by. It is faintly similar in shape, but it is made of cast iron, not brick, and it is a good deal more decorative – 'art nouveau' was how one writer described it.

It looks like part of a traffic control lay-out, but, like Scarty's Monument, it has a much humbler role. It is a ventilator – a gas main ventilator.

3
THE SHIPROW

A key to the ancient Shiprow Port is preserved in a collection of local antiquities at Provost Skene's House in Aberdeen. At one time there were only three Ports (they were also called Gates or Bows), and three silver keys were presented to the Provost on his election, but then there were four – 'There's nae sic anidder in a' the four bows o' Aiberdeen', went an old saying – and finally there were six.

The most important Port was the 'Schip-raw'. Erected at the south end of the road within a few yards of the Shorebrae, it was also known as the Trinity or Quay-head Port because it led to the Trinity Friars' place as well as to the quay. It was removed in the 18th century. These Ports were stone-built archways set in massive stone walls and fitted with two iron-bound and studded doors

The Shiprow was the burgh's main thoroughfare into the city until the building of Marischal Street in 1767. Travellers from the south followed a narrow, awkward route down Windmill Brae to the Bow Brig, then through the Green and up the Shiprow to the Castle.

'The Shiprow', wrote G. M. Fraser in his *Aberdeen Street Names*, 'was the only road that led from the low ground near the shore to the hill-head on which the Castle and the Castlegate came to be situated, so that it has been used as a public highway by countless numbers of all classes through eight centuries'.

In its long life, the Shiprow has had sharply contrasting swings of fortune. It had a noxious past. At one time its citizens were ordered to remove their 'myddings' to get rid of the 'awful stynk' during a Royal visit. It saw a prosperous age when only the elite were drawn to it – wealthy merchants, burgesses and lairds from the neighbouring counties, living in 'tenements' or 'lodgings'. Traders moved into its courts and closes. In the late 19th and early 20th centuries it became a vast slum. Eventually, the demolition men moved in, sweeping away most of its history.

I was pondering on this when I went down the Shiprow. I was thinking particularly of a man who had lived to see almost a century of change in what was known in its early days as the *Vicus Navium*, the Ship Road. He had seen it in its bad years and in its good years

One of the last of the closes in the Shiprow.

and had formed an unassailable attachment to it. I first read his name, Thomas Spark, in an old document drawn up by Alexander W.S. Johnston of Newton Dee in 1860 – 'A Short Memoir of James Young, Merchant Burgess of Aberdeen, and Rachel Cruickshank, his Spouse, and of their Descendants'. James Young's brother was William Young of Sheddocksley, who was Provost of Aberdeen from 1778 to 1779 and 1782 to 1783, and Thomas Spark was 'Clerk to Messrs William and James Young, Merchants in Aberdeen'. A footnote to the memoir said that Spark was subsequently appointed Treasurer and Clerk of Aberdeen Royal Infirmary, a post he held for many years. It then went on – 'Of this respectable individual it has been related that he never for a single night during his long-extended existence slept out of the house in the Shiprow of Aberdeen in which

The Shiprow, looking up towards Exchequer Row, with the Town House in the background

he was born and in which he died, aged 92, in March, 1848, and that he had never been farther from the place of his birth than the parish of Nether Banchory'.

The footnote ended: 'In these days of rapid and easy locomotion such a spirit of adherence to their birthplace may appear to be somewhat remarkable.'

There was another stay-at-home resident mentioned in the Memoir. His name was Ninian Kynoch, and he died at Aberdeen in March, 1846, at the age of 74. He was, said the memoir, 'wont to tell that he had never slept a night out of Aberdeen and had never been at a greater distance from that town than Dunnottar Castle, sixteen or seventeen miles south of Aberdeen; after viewing which, he returned home before night'.

I wondered where the remarkable Mr Spark had lived in the Shiprow. No address was given in the memoir. His home might have been hidden away in one of its courts and closes. The Castlegate had a rabbit warren of closes, but the Shiprow had its share, some with intriguing tales to them. As G.M. Fraser wrote, 'Certain of the Shiprow closes have names that excite interest.' That was written in 1911. Now, sadly, most of the old closes have gone. The entrance to some can be seen on the south end of the Shiprow, but here the street has become tawdry and neglected.

While other old properties fell to the demolition hammer, one court stood firm – Ross's Court. This was the home of John Ross of Arnage, a famous Provost of Aberdeen. When he bought the house he put a new front door on the east front so that he could see from his doorstep his own trading ships in the harbour. Cuthbert Graham, in a historical walk-about of Aberdeen, wrote these lines:

> The Provost stood at the door of his house
> And he counted his ships on the tide,
> And he sailed on a barque to the Low Countrie,
> And in Amsterdam he died.
>
> But the house that he bought and plenished so fine
> Lived on when he was dead,
> And McGibbon and Ross admired its line,
> 'In some respects unique,' they said
> And that was all very fine.
>
> But a graceless age took little care
> Of the house on the Shiprow Brae;
> And what with its years and its wear and tear
> It fell on an evil day.

The Provost had gone to Amsterdam on business and in September 1714 he died there of ague (malarial fever) at the age of forty-nine. He was buried in the English church in Amsterdam. Two centuries later, when his house was in a state of near collapse and ruin, preservationists launched a campaign to save it from that 'graceless age'. The result is that today the house is a splendid museum, with the new Maritime Museum as its neighbour.

There was another Shiprow close called Mearns Court. This had nothing to do with Mearns Street, which was named after Provost Daniel Mearns, who played an important role in clearing up slums in the Shorelands. The Shiprow Mearns was a stocking manufacturer, who travelled with his wares to the Low Counties.

Mearns' son-in-law was Alexander Robertson, supervisor for excise for the Aberdeen district. Here, there is an interesting link with that legendary gauger, Malcolm Gillespie. Gillespie was one of Robertson's officers and their relationship was so close that the supervisor's son often spent his holiday with Gillespie at Crombie Cottage, Skene.

There was a tragic end to Gillespie's career. To clear his debts, which he said were incurred by employing too many assistants, he forged twenty-two different bills. The law caught up with him and at a sitting of the Aberdeen Circuit Court he was sentenced to be hanged on 16 October 1827. In the week that he was executed his daughter, Jane Maxwell Gordon, who was named after the famous Duchess of Gordon, stayed with Alexander Robertson in his house at Mearns Court.

4
SUPERMAN AND THE BIG HOLE

Aberdeen has always been proud of its Big Hole. The Granite City grew out of it – a 480-feet-deep pit which for 200 years yielded up the glittering stone that made buildings and bridges all over the world. People came from far and wide to see it. They stood on a small ramshackle wooden platform on the edge of the quarry and peered nervously down into what the writer Nigel Tranter once called 'a quite terrifying man-made abyss'.

To one man this great hole was to have a special fascination. His name was Charles Ludwig. Born in 1911, one of a family of nine children, he was taught at the Grammar School before going to Aberdeen University in 1929 to study Medicine. He was a brilliant student, graduating MBChB with honours in 1934 and winning the Murray Gold Medal as the most distinguished graduate of the year. He went on to become a Lecturer in Physiology at Leeds University.

But the scholarly mask hid another Charles Ludwig – a man restless for adventure, reaching out for new challenges, new achievements. He might have been regarded by some as rash, sometimes foolhardy, but his friends said he was neither. Long after his death, Alan Morgan, one of his contemporaries at school and university, wrote of him: 'He was the nearest to a Superman that I ever knew personally.'

His attention to his studies was matched by his dedication to sport. He played a prominent part in the University's athletic life, making his mark as a cross-country runner. His main interest, however, was mountaineering. He became a junior member of the Cairngorm Club in 1924 while still at the Grammar School and soon built up a reputation for himself. In 1933 he carried off a climb that put his name in the record books – the first solo ascent of the notorious Douglas-Gibson Gully on Lochnagar.

The gully was named after two climbers, William Douglas and J. H. Gibson, who in March 1893 got within 1500 feet of the top and then had to turn back. The late Tom Patey wrote about Ludwig's climb in *One Man's Mountains*. Ludwig, he said, set little store upon his Douglas Gully adventure, but his success encouraged later generations of young climbers to try it. 'So for a time in the bad old days "before the dawn of reason",' wrote Patey, 'many young tigers were blooded in "Gibson's", often literally.'

Ludwig also climbed in Skye and the north-west Highlands, getting there by bicycle. He displayed a touch of eccentricity on some of his expeditions, as, for instance, when he returned from one of his trips to the west. Having covered 264 miles, he decided to cycle out to Banchory and back, a distance of sixteen miles, so that his total mileage would be in round figures.

His eccentricity was also seen in the clothes he wore for his climbs – drill shorts, an assortment of pullovers, and a pair of tennis shoes. His unorthodox dress had no effect on his climbing; his ambition was to climb all the 300 'Munros' in Scotland and he succeeded in doing over 250 of them.

In December, 1931, he carried out one of his most unusual climbs – a notorious 'first'. This climb, however, didn't take place in the hills, but in the heart of Aberdeen. With his friend Donald Dawson he climbed the Mitchell Tower at Marsichal College and fixed to it 'a weird pyjama-clad effigy crowned by a human skull and wearing a lum hat'. On the morning of Wednesday 9 December, the *Press and Journal* carried a big picture of the tower and its 'skeleton'. Prominent headlines read:

MARISCHAL MYSTERY

DARE-DEVIL PRANK OF STUDENT

DUMMY FIXED ON TOP OF TOWER

'From the weather-vane of Aberdeen's highest spire, the Mitchell Tower of Marischal College,' the *P&J* reported, 'there gazed forth upon the city yesterday at an altitude of 235 feet a grotesque effigy. Onlookers pondered and puzzled over the fact that "It" wore a tile hat.

'Many speculations were made regarding the "identity" of the weird apparition. Was it a painter, a plumber or a steeplejack? Was it some strange black-headed white-feathered bird of passage that had come to rest?

'A facetious fellow suggested that it looked like Ghandi blessing the town.

'It was revealed that the head was a human skull topped by a "lum" hat, that it wore a suit of pyjamas, and had long, thin dangling legs.'

The towering granite face of Rubislaw Quarry.

The paper wondered who had endangered his life by such a prank, and the next morning it asked, 'Who will take it down?' A week later 'The Old Man of Marischal', as the *P&J* called it, was removed by two slaters. It had, said the *Journal*, been a seven-day wonder, viewed by thousands of citizens. Country folk had even travelled into town to see it.

It was learned later that Ludwig had prepared a black outfit with a skeleton painted on it and had planned to don it and climb down to meet the steeeplejacks who would come up to remove it. This final stunt was foiled when he went up in the early morning and found that the trap door into the upper chamber of the tower had been locked.

Ludwig was involved in a number of other student stunts. In one charity event he and another student dressed up as apes, climbed up a rone pipe on top of the North Bank (now the Archibald Simpson restaurant at the corner of King Street and Union Street) and rattled their collection tins at passers-by. In another Gala Week caper he careered down Marischal Street on a bicycle and went straight into the harbour.

But his greatest escapade outdid all the others. In December, 1931, he became Aberdeen's 'Blondin', the first man to challenge the Big Hole. In those days, Rubislaw Quarry lay open to the public, a magnet for student stuntmen, like the anonymous student who lit a cigarette and sang while suspended over the awesome drop, or the students who hung an Aberdeen Charities Banner over it in April 1966.

Ludwig blazed the trail for them. He crossed the quarry, hand over hand, on the wire used to bring great blocks of granite up from its rocky bed 480 feet below. It was a feat that stood comparison with that of another high-wire stuntman with the same first name – Charles Blondin, who crossed Niagara Falls on a tightrope. The Blondin wires on which Ludwig made his daredevil crossing of the quarry were named after him.

What made Charles Ludwig risk his life in this crazy fashion? Did he court publicity? Was he simply a show-off? Alan Morgan, the school friend who had likened him to Superman, said he was neither a madcap nor a show off. 'He had an especial sort of bravery that carefully assessed all the risks while deliberately courting danger,' said Morgan. 'I am not philosopher enough to know why.'

In 1940, Ludwig volunteered for service in the RAF. He could have

A dramatic aerial view of Rubislaw Quarry.

become a medical officer, but he joined as an ordinary aircraftman so that he could fly. He was commissioned in 1941. In January 1942, the month he was due to be married to the daughter of a professor at Leeds, he was killed on a mission over Germany. He was thirty years old. Donald Dawson, who in September 1933 made a notable ascent of the Mitre Ridge of Beinn a' Bhuird with Ludwig, also died in the war.

Rubislaw Quarry was closed in 1970. Today, the citizens of Aberdeen are not allowed to take a peep at the hole which gave them their city and helped to put it on the international map. The quarry is shut off from the outside world by wooden fences. Large yellow 'Danger' notices warn would-be Ludwigs to keep out. For nearly thirty years it has lain untouched while arguments have raged backwards and forwards over what should be done with it.

There has been no shortage of ideas. A nuclear bomb shelter, a jail, a hospital site, a large deep-freeze, a zoo, a cable-car system carrying visitors across the quarry to a restaurant, a granite museum . . . these were among the proposals put forward by newspaper readers. One wit suggested that the whole thing should be turned upside down and used as an artifical ski slope, while another thought that the ugly eyesore of St Nicholas House, with its municipal offices, should be dropped into it.

Aberdeen District Council wanted to carry out a feasibility study on the use of the quarry for refuse disposal, but the idea brought a storm of protest. One local poet, who regarded the proposal as 'high treason', said the east end of the city could keep its stink and pollution:

> We toffs that live up Queen's Road way,
> Adjacent to the quarry,
> Are not like other common clay,
> We're not Tom, Dick or Harry.
>
> So common folk their lot must thole,
> Don't envy us our luck;
> Just leave as with our empty hole,
> And you can have the muck.

From a woman reader, Anne Flann, came a proposal that would have warmed Charles Ludwig's heart. 'Rubislaw quarry has a rugged, hard granite face', she wrote. 'What better use than to turn it into a school for climbers? It would bring more people to our city. It would contribute to the lessening of untutored climbers climbing our hills and placing other lives at risk in the process. It would still remain a tourist attraction, but with the added benefit of serving a useful purpose.'

Nothing came of this or any other proposal. The quarry still lies empty and deserted, with nothing to show that it was this 'man-made abyss' that gave birth to the Granite City.

5
THE GARGOYLE

Among the maze of lanes and closes in the centre of Aberdeen in the 17th century there was a short street called Ragg's Lane. It was connected to the Guestrow, although it was said to be a good deal less respectable than its neighbour. In time, its name was changed to Baillie Ragg's Wynd, which may have been an attempt to upgrade it socially.

The man who gave his name to Ragg's Lane was Alexander Ragg, a prosperous merchant, who served as a magistrate from 1697 to 1701. Baillie Ragg died in 1719. His tombstone lay at one time in the middle of the front churchyard of St Nicholas, but was moved to the front of the west door.

For countless years the boots of generations of visitors to St Nicholas have tramped over the Baillie's grave, obliterating the inscription. To find out what it said you have to dig out a series of sketches of the St Nicholas slabs which are held in the Aberdeen central library.

Now the Baillie has gone and Ragg's Lane has gone, and there is nothing left to remind you that there ever was such a place – except a dour, ugly face. The face, dark and bearded, appeared on a gargoyle that was set up on a wall at the corner of Ragg's Lane by the owner of the property, George Russel. Edward Meldrum, who drew a sketch of it in his book *Aberdeen of Old*, said it was 'very similar to the cast-iron faces found, with projecting water-pipe, at the mouth of the town's old wells'.

Russel was an eccentric who fell out with one of his neighbours in Queen Street. His animosity made him sculpt his neighbour's head and build it into the corner of Ragg's Lane, about 4.5 m (15 feet) above the pavement. Every time his neighbour came to Ragg's Lane this grotesque gargoyle of his face stared at him from the wall.

What Baillie Ragg would have thought about it nobody can tell. Russel was born in 1810, nearly a century after the Baillie's death. But the gargoyle sculptor could not have been all bad, for when he died he directed in his will that annual payments of money should be made to the city's police constables and the local scaffies.

The gargoyle on the gable of Provost Skene's house.

The gargoyle was left to scowl at passers-by until the building was demolished in 1959. Today, it is stuck on the gable of Provost Skene's House, out of the public gaze. There is nothing to tell people who *do* notice it why it is there, or who it was – or why its owner looks so angry and disgruntled.

6

THE BLACK FAST DAY

When you stand on the Victoria Bridge between Market Street and Torry, watching the River Dee swirling away to the sea, there is nothing to tell you of the terrible events that took place there on Wednesday 5 April 1876. On that day thirty-two people were drowned when the ferry-boat linking Torry with the city capsized. Forty-two were saved.

Why did it happen? Could it have been avoided? Who were the people responsible for the tragedy?

To find the answer to these questions you have to go back to what became known as the Black Fast Day – the day of the half-yearly Sacramental Fast, when all Aberdeen was on holiday. There was no bridge then and from early morning the ferry plied backwards and forwards, carrying hundreds of people across the Dee to enjoy the day on the breezy slopes of Torry.

It was a clear, balmy day. Penny shows and shooting galleries had been set up and public houses were doing a roaring trade. But, although the sun shone, the river was dangerously full, heavily swollen by the rapid thawing of snow in the Deeside hills. For the previous day or two the current had been fast-running, so much so that on the Tuesday the tacksman of the ferry-boat had refused to operate it. The ferrying was done by a wire rope, fixed on each bank of the river, which passed along the length of the boat and doubled over a wheel in the centre. The wheel was turned by the ferrymen.

The holiday crowds were difficult to control. When the boat touched the Aberdeen shore about three o'clock in the afternoon, passengers jumping out had to push through the crowd waiting to board it. Meanwhile, the Torry-bound passengers forced their way on to the boat before it was emptied. One young girl was unable to get out and had to return with the boat. She was drowned.

There were different reports on the numbers on board the ferry; one official said there were over forty, another said there were fifty-one, and spectators on the shore gave estimates of sixty, seventy, and even eighty. When it was all over and the roll of missing people was completed it was found that there had been at least seventy-seven people in the boat.

The ferryman in charge of the boat was a William Masson, who was assisted by a married man called John Mitchell. Masson left the boat just as it was filled. He said later that Mitchell had asked him to get a glass of water, but when he came back the boat had gone and had drifted into the stream. Others who were there told a different story – they heard him say that the boat was overcrowded and he wouldn't risk his life on it.

When the boat set off across the river its gunwale was only an inch or two from the water. One small boy was seen playing with his bonnet in the water. Out in mid-stream, the current began to make itself felt and the tension on the wire rope increased. The boat stopped, the rope stretched taut from bank to bank. It began to cant to one side and water poured into it. Suddenly, the sky was filled with the shrieks and screams of terrified passengers as the boat began to submerge. Turning downstream, it tilted over.

Horrified spectators on the shore, watching as the ferry turned bottom up, saw some of the passengers leaping into the water. Six or seven young men and a woman were able to grab hold of it and floated down river with it to safety. Within minutes – it seemed like hours to the onlookers – four small boats were launched from the Torry side, and one from the Aberdeen side, while a second ferry boat lying nearby joined in the rescue. They were able to save thirty people.

A pamphlet, 'Catastrophe on the River Dee', was published on the day after the disaster by the *Aberdeen Free Press,* the proceeds going to a Relief Fund that had been set up. Some of the rescues were described in the pamphlet as 'wonderful and miraculous'. Two fishermen, Alexander Craig and his father-in-law, Alexander Caie, sen., were standing on the beach at Torry when the ferryboat was loaded. Craig, who was waiting for his wife to return from the city, saw her board the boat, a creel on her back. He had a premonition that something was wrong and shouted to her not to get into the boat. He was too late.

The two men launched a boat and made for the ferry, which careened over just as they reached it. Craig's wife, who was thrown into the water, was being pulled under by other passengers who had grabbed hold of her creel. She was in danger of being strangled as well as drowned, but her husband caught her just as she was going under. Between them, the two men also rescued about a dozen other people.

Williamina Strachan, a girl from the Gallowgate, was rescued by her own father. He had been over on the Torry side, heard her cries for help and saw her floating past in the river. A Mrs Farquhar, from Jute Street, was pulled out by a fisher's wife at the Torry side. She was still clinging tenaciously to her thirteen-month-old baby, who was lying quietly in her arms. Her daughter, Jessie, who had been with her, was picked up by a boat. Two sisters, Mary Ann and Elizabeth Simpson, were saved by different boats, one on the Torry side, the other on the Footdee side. Each thought the other had been drowned.

Fate played some peculiar tricks on that dreadful day. Of four men who were together on the ferry, only one was saved, but among another group of the same size it was the other way round – one was drowned and the remaining three were saved.

There was a comical side to some of the rescues. A 'one-legged' man called Hogg (the description said he had one good leg and 'a bit of one'), jumped from the boat before it capsized. He began to swim towards the Torry side, but suddenly realised that he had left his crutch. He immediately turned round and swam back, and actually succeeded in getting it. When he finally made it to the shore he complained that he had lost half of a flute which he had taken with him to play among the rocks at Torry.

George C. Selbie and his sister, Margaret, were on board the ferry. When it sank, George tried to save his sister, but missed her and brought another girl ashore instead. He landed on the shore with a gold watch in his mouth! It had belonged to his father and he had put it in his mouth so that he wouldn't lose it while swimming to safety.

James Brown, mate of the Aberdeen schooner *Speed*, was in a pleasure boat with his wife and family when the accident happened. He landed his wife and family and with the help of two fishermen went out and rescued five people from drowning. Thirteen or fourteen salmon fishers left their work and saved a number of lives. They then dragged the river and harbour entrance, looking for bodies, but without success.

A Gordon Hospital lad named Harte, who had gone to Torry on a Fast Day outing, was hauled ashore unconscious. He was still holding in his clenched fist the ha'penny for his return trip to the city.

Lord Provost George Jamieson and most of the magistrates and councillors were at the scene of the tragedy, making arrangements for the rescued victims. Caps and bonnets were laid out for identification and wives and mothers rushed about looking for news of their relatives. That evening, thousands of people converged on Fittie, others crowded the street in front of the police office hoping to get some information.

Lists of those lost and saved were issued on the day following the disaster, Among those saved was 'Patrick Harte (13) – Gordon's Hospital boy – son of Widow Harte, residing at 56 Regent Quay' and 'George Selbie, residing in Gallowgate – sister drowned'. The list of those lost made heartbreaking reading. For instance, George Dickie, a 27-year-old stonecutter who left a widow and three children, had told his wife that he was going out for a walk and would be home by tea-time. He had refused to go on an earlier boat because he thought it was overloaded.

James Munro, a 40-year-old foundry labourer, 29 Shuttle Lane, left a widow and seven children. He had recently married his wife, who had been a widow with five children. Two children were born later. Both husband and wife were on the boat. 'After they submerged in the water', said the *Free Press* report, 'her husband continued to "grip hold" of her hand for some time, till at length his grasp relaxed and she saw him no more. She got on to the bottom of the boat and was rescued from that.'

Robert Badger (23), a seaman and labourer living with his parents at the Links Battery, went over to Torry on the ferry with his young brother, John Alexander. 'The little lad did not see his brother when the boat capsized,' it was reported. 'The only person he saw was "the man with the cripple leg" who swam ashore.'

The case of 13-year-old Jessie M'Condach was said to be 'the saddest of all these sad cases'. Jessie worked as a message girl with a firm in Park Road. She had been over in Torry on the morning and had to get back to the city to pick up her employers' letters at the Post Office at half-past four. 'She had entered the boat at Torry side and come across with it. The unfortunate girl, however, never got out of the boat owing to the great crush that there was to get into it, and consequently she was taken back by the boat, and thus met her death.'

The recovery of the bodies went on in the days that followed. 'Creepers' used in trawling were brought in to the search. They consisted of a long iron rods with cords attached, each bearing two or three strong hooks. Twenty trawlers were used in this operation, lining up between Point Law and Abercromby's Jetty and working their way towards the North Pier. Thirty minutes after the operation began the body of a young man was pulled to the surface.

Ninety minutes later fifteen bodies had been recovered. One of the trawlers brought to the surface three young lads clasped in each others arms. One slipped into the water again, but was recovered. All the bodies were laid out on the floor of the bath-house. 'There was nothing whatever repulsive about the spectacle,' said the *Free Press* pamphlet. 'In fact, but for the dripping clothes, the tangled hair,and the clammy, water-sucked hands, there would have been somewhat of a mournfully attractive appearance about the dead.

'The girl Jessie M'Condach looked more like a waxen figure than anything else. She had a beautifully fresh complexion and a sweet smile lighted up her handsome features. By her side lay a pleasant-featured little boy, who had all the appearance of being wrapped in healthy and refreshing sleep.'

The boy, Duncan, had been given fourpence from his mother before leaving his house on the day of the disaster. He apparently spent a penny before reaching the boat and then paid the boat fare with another halfpenny. 'The remaining coppers', said the report, 'were found firmly clasped in the right hand of the corpse.'

A week after the tragedy a number of unclaimed articles lay in the city police office. The list included 'Four felt hats (stiff), all men's sizes; two Balmoral or Glengarry bonnets, broad and flat-topped; two peaked cloth caps, boys' sizes; imitation sealskin cap, much worn; two boys' bonnets (worsted); one cloth cap with flaps and strings (picked up in Bay of Nigg on Monday, and may not be connected with the Ferry-boat accident)'. A light bamboo cane and 'several small articles such as worsted cuffs and bits of girls' dresses' were also on show.

William Shelley, an Aberdeen police sergeant with a reputation as a poet, wrote a poem called 'Are There Any Bodies Found?' and donated the profits to the Relief Fund. Shelley's poem was one of many that flooded into the local newspapers. One poem by Arthur Mitchell, a builder, stood out from the rest because of its title – 'A Brig to Torry'. It was a subject that was on everyone's lips, for after the disaster the Aberdeen Land Association made an offer of £4000 towards the building of a bridge on the line of Market Street.

Mitchell's poem, which mentioned the £4000 offer, was more than a call for a new bridge. It also pointed the finger at the guilty men who in the past had held up such a project by 'party-faction plots':

The Victoria Bridge, built after the ferry disaster.

> Think not of plotting, selfish men.
> Whose sordid wish is all for gain,
> Whose only care is but their ain,
> And no' a Brig to Torry.

They would look to Balnagask for money – 'On a' the lairds we'll make a raid' – and they would keep an eye on the Baker Lairds of Kincorth – 'The thousands here who eat their bread say, "Mind our Brig to Torry".' What was wealth to laird or king, asked Mitchell, if it didn't bring man's respect. He had a special message for tight-fisted Aberdonians:

> Greedy, grasping, selfish sots,
> Who keep their pennies, pounds and groats,
> They're little better than the stots –
> Just drown them a' at Torry.

'It will be a fitting memorial to those whose sad fate it was to be drowned on the river on the Black Fast-Day of 1876', said the *Free Press*. Five years after the disaster the Victoria Bridge was finally opened. Today, the only reminder of what happened there more than a century ago are street names on either side of the river – Ferry Road and Ferry Place.

7
THE GYPES

A foolish awkward person, a silly ass, a lout – that is the dictionary definition of a gype. Nowadays it is a word that is rarely heard or used. Gypes have become an endangered species, kept alive by the works of Doric poets like Charles Murray and the Peterhead fisher-poet Peter Buchan. Peter wrote about a fisher quine, Kirsty, who was 'a silly gypit craitur', and Murray used the word in a First-World-War poem called 'Fae France'. In it, he wrote about a soldier who refused to leave an officer who had been wounded. The Lieutenant cursed him for a fool:

> 'Ging on an' leave me here, ye gype,
> an' make yer feet yer freen,
> 'Na, na', says I, 'ye brocht me here,
> I'm nae gaun hame my leen'.

There were plenty of gypes in Aberdeen in the early 19th century. So much so, in fact, that one of the city's most curious societies was formed – the Gype Society. The man behind it was Alexander Robb, a local tailor, Deacon of the Tailor Incorporation, and a well-known versifier. He brought together a number of young tradesmen interested in amateur drama and formed a club under what he himself admitted was 'a somewhat ridiculous title'. His only excuse was that it would prevent anyone else from giving it an even worse name.

The society staged three plays during the winter, with relatives making up most of the audience. Each member contributed a penny a week towards expenses and Deacon Robb wrote a song or an epilogue that was sung or spoken after the performance. The songs usually criticised the performers by name, so Robb decided that most of them were unfit for publication.

Some, however, *were* published, 'more as curiosities than as having any merit', and among them was 'The Gypes' Frolic'. The performer, who was dressed in the character of a fool or gype, set out to show that there were gypes the world over. Alexander the Great was a gype, gypes laid Troy in ashes, Socrates was 'sair gypit', and there weren't any greater gypes than Antony and Cleopatra.

There were gypes among lawyers and doctors, merchants and tradesmen, nobles and gentry – 'an' even some gypes hae been parsons'. As for masons, they were respectable enough in their lodges:

> But when they parade on the streets,
> Wi' their sashes and aprons symbolic,
> The Bible an' a' their regalia,
> Oh, then comes the gypical frolic!

The society performed a play called 'The Duel', in which a Baron and a Count had 'a fearfu' kick-up'. The Count threatened to pull the Baron's snout and kick his doup, but eventually they decided to settle their differences with firearms:

> Then name your arms an' time to yoke,
> An' name the field o' glory.
> Pistols – the morn, at five o'clock,
> Upon the hills o' Torry.

The Gype Society lasted for many years, but eventually faded away. Deacon Robb died in 1859 at the age of seventy-eight. Fifteen years before his death, another club with cultural ambitions disappeared from the city's social scene. Like the Gype Society, its members were people with literary, dramatic and musical interests.

'The Acorn Club' took its name from a tap-room in Huxter Row called the Royal Oak. It was run by Tom Denham, a one-time bootmaker, poet and singer – a 'rollicking blade' who was always ready for 'one bottle more'. Not surprisingly, the members of the Acorn Club all had 'a fair drouth'. They took the view that there should be 'a minimum of solid washed down by a maximum of liquid'.

The club, however, had a brief existence and Tom Denham ended up heavily in debt. He published some of his poems and prose, including a crude sketch called 'The Nose'. In it, he considered a variety of noses – 'Greek, Roman, pug, aquiline, bony, greasy, prickly, turned-up, turned-down and turned-aside'. Finally, there was 'the weeping willow-nose':

> From whose sharp tips the pearlet flows,
> When winter sends her frosts and snows.

The critics and public dismissed it in one word – 'Nauseous'. The result was that Denham went off to America and was never heard of again.

The club tradition was firmly established in the 19th century, when, according to George Walker in *Aberdeen Awa'*, a book of sketches published in 1897, all ranks and classes 'formed themselves into congenial coteries; they met in inns at all seasons and hours'. He named a number of Friendly Societies among the merrymakers – 'Shipmasters, Wigmakers, Dyers, Independent Friends, True Blue Gardeners and others'. There was a Philosophical Society, originally founded under the name of the Wise Club, and there was even 'a demonaic society' called the Hell-Fire Club.

If anyone had expected the Town Council to show a shining example they would have been disappointed. There was a song that might well have been written today, when people are complaining about our City Fathers wining and dining and using up the cash in the Common Good Fund. It went like this:

> In guid times auld, when days were cauld,
> Wi' sleet an' sna' an' a' that,
> The Council board was aye weel stored
> Wi' something nice, an' a' that,
> An' a' that, an' a' that;
> Aft Baillies spak' wi' draps o' that
> Like Solomons, an' a' that.

If Deacon Robb had lived to see the curious clubs and societies formed in Aberdeen in the 20th century he might have thought it still had enough gypes to take their place alongside Socrates and Alexander the Great. At any rate, the Sit-Siccar Society would have interested him because of its preoccupation with doups.

Charles Murray formed the Sit-Siccar Society with a few close friends and associates when he returned to the North-east on his retirement from South Africa. Two Governors-General, John Buchan, Lord Tweedsmuir and Sir Patrick Duncan were active members.

Murray wrote a poem, 'Advice to the Sit-Siccars', urging them to sit siccar (sit tight) and keep a calm sough:

> In love or in liquor
> In case 'at ye coup
> Be wise an' sit siccar
> Ye're safe on your doup.

Another group must have listened to his advice, for they called themselves 'The Calm Soughers'. Its members were a number of

Aberdeen doctors who met at weekends in a well-known temperance hotel, the Kilmarnock Arms, in Cruden Bay.

Murray also had a connection with the Life Preservers' Society. Life preservers were short clubs used for self-defence against criminals, but the Life Preservers' Society was set up to fight a different kind of enemy – overwork and bad health. The man behind it was William Tawse, a prominent Scottish works contractor, who felt that businessmen should be out walking in the fresh air at weekends instead of sitting desk-bound in their offices.

There were twenty members. Every Saturday they met at some starting point thirty to forty miles from the town and walked through the country by a disused road, path or hillside; the average length of the walk was about twelve miles. They chalked up well over 200 walks . . . across the bleak moors of the Cabrach, around Loch Muick, up Lochnagar and over the top of Ben Avon to see the sunrise.

Deacon Robb would probably have placed them at the top of his Gype list. He preferred people to exercise their lungs at the bachelor soirees he organised in the Adelphi, where they could . . .

> . . . join in the sang, then the glee or the chorus
> As lang an' as loud as ye like, ane an' a',
> Till the folk in the Adelphi, while hearin' the roar o's,
> Will wonder what's happenin' in Bachelors' Ha'.

Nearly half a century after Deacon Robb's death, another bachelor club was set up. This was the Aberdeen Bachelor and Benedict Club, founded on 14 February 1903 by a few businessmen who had come into Aberdeen from the country and wanted to meet, wine and dine, and share their thoughts on the issues of the day. A benedict is a confirmed bachelor who, like Benedick in Shakespeare's *Much Ado About Nothing*, suddenly changes his mind and finds himself a wife.

Their motto is *Vinculis Concordia*, indicating wine and harmony. I was a member of the club for a time. It is still flourishing, even if there are no longer any bachelors *or* benedicts on the roll. I have sometimes wondered if the twelfth clause in the club's constitution was ever enforced – 'In the event of any member of the Club taking unto himself a wife, he shall remit to the Treasurer forthwith one guinea.'

The club has a limited number of meetings at which one member, following the stated aim of 'intellectual advancement', talks on a subject of his choice, followed by discussion. They also have an annual dinner, when their ranks are swollen by guests. Turning the clock back, they sing the good old songs – 'as lang and as loud as they like' – and their voices can be heard almost as far away as the old Bachelors' Ha' in the Adelphi. Their favourite song, often called for at the dinner, is 'Lucky Jim'.

Oddly enough, 'Lucky Jim' is also the theme song of the F.R.S. Club, which is a kind of male keep-fit, weight-watching club with social overtones. The club was founded in 1935, when a group of men met for keep-fit sessions in a garage in Raeburn Place, winding it up with a shower under a cold-water wash-bed on the garage floor. It required the same sort of stamina shown by the city's Sea Dookers – all-the-year-round sea bathers who dip in the briny whatever the weather or temperature. Deacon Robb would certainly have regarded *them* as gypes!

The initials F.R.S. stand for Fellows of the Right Sort, but this high-sounding title is really a cover-up, for there are a number of alternatives; for instance, 'Frolicking, Rollicking Sportsmen' and 'Found Rarely Sober'. One familiar title, however, goes to the heart of the matter, or, more accurately, to the stomach. The real meaning of the letters F.R.S., I was told, is Forty Roon the Stomach.

8
DRY LINES, NO FISH

A huge boulder with a curious inscription cut into it stands on the south bank of the River Dee at Craigendinnie, near Aboyne. The inscription reads DRY LINES. NO FISH. How it came to be there, and what it means, is a story that goes back to the days when an eccentric Englishman called William Cunliffe Brooks was laird of Glen Tanar.

His initials, WCB, are stamped on stones, wells and seats all over the estate, along with cryptic homilies urging passers-by to 'Drink Thank, Think' or to remember that 'Honest water never left man in the mire'. The Craigendinnie stone, which is almost 6 ft long and 3 ft wide, had WCB's mark on it. Today it is hidden away from the public eye and seen mostly by fishers casting their lines in the Dee.

Cunliffe Brooks was an enthusiastic fisher. When he returned from a trip away from home he always wanted to know how the fish had been biting on the Glen Tanar beats. One of his ghillies was a man called Boatie Stephen, who got the nickname because he operated the ferry that once plied across the Dee about a quarter of a mile below the present bridge at Dinnet.

DRY LINES, NO FISH – the stone.

W. Cunliffe Brooks (centre) out on the moors with a house party.

When a new railway station was built at Aboyne in 1896, Cunliffe Brooks built a coach house for his own use in the Station Square. This building, with Brooks' own distinctive architectural style, can still be seen beside Strachan's store. At one end the initials, WCB, are carved out on the wall.

It was there that his coachman waited for him when he returned by train from trips to the south. On one occasion, driving down to Glen Tanar, Cunliffe Brooks met 'Boatie' Stephen coming up from the river at Craigendinnie. He was carrying his fishing rod.

'Well, Boatie,' said the laird, 'have you caught any salmon?'

'Na! Na!' said Boatie. 'Not one! There's nae fish there the day.'

They chatted for a few minutes and then Cunliffe Brooks went on his way. Later, he gave instructions through his factor that 'Boatie' wasn't to come to the river again until he got further orders.

Boatie was eventually told to go back and fish on the Craigendinnie beat. He found the laird waiting for him. Things had changed since his last visit. A beautiful walk had been made down to the riverside and a big stone wall had been built around a massive stone lying at the foot of a larch tree. The wall was semi-circular in shape, looking almost like a giant pulpit, and that's what it came to be known as – the Pulpit. There was a steep drop down to the river

The Pulpit.

and on the west side of the wall there was a wrought-iron gate. From the Pulpit you looked up the Dee to the distant hills.

But it was the big stone that caught Boatie's eye. It was the stone he had lain out on for a snooze the last time he had been at Craigendinnie – on the day he had told the laird there were no fish in the Dee. Now a cryptic message had been cut out on the stone – DRY LINES, NO FISH.

'Now Boatie,' said Cunliffe Brooks, 'that's to commemorate the day that you met me on the road to Craigendinnie.' He then told Boatie, 'You were never fishing that day – because your line was dry.' The sharp-eyed laird had noticed that his ghillie's fishing line had no water on it. And, as the message on the stone said, if there were dry lines there were no fish. Boatie had been sleeping on duty.

It was Jimmy Oswald, former head keeper on Glen Tanar, now retired, who told me the story of Boatie Stephen and the Craigendinnie stone. He heard it from Charlie Milne, a ghillie at Glen Tanar, and Charlie got it from his father, John Milne, who was a noted ghillie on the estate.

John Milne, said Jimmy, was 'shot dead up the Allachy' in an accident. It happened up the Knockie Branar – 'little hill of the place of tangled roots', say the place-name experts. Fir roots are in the peat around this hill south of Pannanich. John was only thirty-seven when he died.

The gate built by W. Cunliffe Brooks on the site.

There is no beautiful walk down to the Craigendinnie stone nowadays. Few people see it, but fishers going down there have Cunliffe Brooks' message at their feet – DRY LINES, NO FISH.

This eccentric laird had other curiosities scattered about his estate. There was, for instance, Wilcebe Road. This was a farm road which he named after himself – Will C.B. – and along it are seven wells, each carrying a message from the laird. One is called the Snakeswell, taking its name from the inscription 'The worm of the still is still the deadliest snake on the hill'.

Another Glen Tanar curiosity is the Haunted Stag, or, at any rate, two stone pillars that mark the spot where it died. Cunliffe Brooks gave the deer its 'haunted' tag because it always eluded him, but one day in 1867 he got it in his sights and brought it down. He put up two stone pillars on the spot, with two stone balls on top marking the distance at which he shot the stag – 267 ft (81 m). It was regarded as no mean feat in those days.

I remember going to the ballroom of Glen Tanar house with Jimmy Oswald to look at some 500 sets of antlers that decorated the ceiling, most of them with the name of the hunter and the date that the deer was shot. We were looking for the Haunted Stag's antlers, but we never found them.

9

A LADY IN A BOX

They called it the Burkin' Hoose. It stood in Aberdeen's Hospital Row, better known today as St Andrews Street, and it took its nickname from the notorious Edinburgh body-snatchers, Burke and Hare, who murdered about thirty people in their search for corpses for medical dissection. The man who paid for the bodies was a distinguished anatomist, Dr Robert Knox, whose name was chanted in a well-known Auld Reekie rhyme:

> Burke an' Hare
> Fell doon the stair
> Wi' a leddy in a box
> Gaun tae Doctor Knox

People who lived in Hospital Row suspected that there might be 'a leddy in a box', or worse, in Aberdeen, in the premises occupied by a lecturer in anatomy, Andrew Moir. Their fears were well-founded, for Moir became the central figure in a Burkin' scandal that swept through the city in the early 1830s.

But the so-called 'resurrectionists' were making their gory mark long before that. The plundering of graves was under way at the turn of the century. In December, 1808, Aberdeen was shocked by its first 'leddy in a box' – the corpse of an old woman called Janet Young, dug from its grave by resurrectionists in St Fittick's churchyard at Nigg. Pieces of a coffin lid and tattered strips of linen lay on ground stained by blood.

Two months later, body-snatchers were disturbed while robbing another grave at Nigg. They buried the corpse in the sand on the north side of the bay, but a storm washed it up on the south side and it was found by relatives. The leader of the body-snatchers was a medical student, who fled the country.

In 1801, another medical student, Charles Jameson, was convicted of stealing a body from the Spital churchyard. It turned out that he was secretary of the Aberdeen Medical Society, which later became the Aberdeen Medico-Chirurgical Society. Set up in 1789 by a group of medical students, it was to all intents and purposes a body-snatching organisation.

The student founders were headed by James McGrigor, later Sir James, who founded the Army Medical Corps. It was McGrigor who led discussions on the need for anatomical instruction in the city. In 1794, the Medical Society received a letter from six former members in London expressing regret that 'dissections have been so long neglected in Aberdeen'. Bodies were procured in London for dissection almost every day, they said. 'We leave anyone to form their opinion whether it would not be an easier affair at Aberdeen.'

It took some time before the Aberdeen students acted, and when they did it was with considerable caution. In 1808, after a serious leakage of information about their activities, it was decided that anyone who betrayed the secrets of the Society had forfeited his word of honour and would be immediately expelled. In 1806, a court case resulted from the discovery of a man's body in the society's hall in King Street. The body was returned to the Spital burial ground at night and when the case came before the court a fine of one guinea was imposed. The Sheriff, whose sympathies lay with the student doctors, suggested that it should be handed to the widow 'to stop her clamour'.

Members of the society were all expected to take their share in body-snatching; those who shirked their duty were fined, but those who were successful in obtaining a 'subject' were given half a guinea. The man who led many of the resurrection raids was Andrew Moir, a gifted lecturer who had originally intended to join the Church. He lectured, demonstrated and dissected in Aberdeen for three years.

Moir, who was highly popular with his students, had rooms in Flourmill Brae and the Guestrow, where he had his home. Tales of the Burke and Hare affair in Edinburgh filtered up to Aberdeen, fueling fears that 'Burkin'' had come to Aberdeen. Stones were frequently flung at the doors and windows of the anatomist's house and visitors were pelted with garbage.

Moir, in need of better accommodation for his work, built an anatomical theatre in St Andrew Street. This was the building that became known as the Burkin' Hoose. It was said that Moir paid too little attention to the feelings of the public, or to his own safety, when he moved into the theatre and began dissecting corpses obtained through grave-robbing. Rumours spread and fears grew.

William Buchanan, in his *Glimpses of Olden Days in Aberdeen* in

1870, told of wild stories that circulated in the city. All kinds of tales were heard, he declared, some true, some imaginary. It was said that a doctor had been seen entering the College-gate in a gig with a lady beside him. But the lady was no lady. 'It was no other than a corpse dressed up as a ruse to deceive the public,' wrote Buchanan. 'Someone who saw the gig declared that the lady was a corpse. It went round the town like lightning and a great concourse of people assembled round the College-gate and threatened a breach of the peace.'

Francis Clerihew, a local advocate, also described in the *Aberdeen Magazine* how the public became increasingly alarmed at the body-snatchers' activities. 'The dread of the Doctors soon became such that neither woman nor child would venture without doors after nightfall,' he wrote. 'In this state of matters no one can wonder that an explosion should take place, and it did take place with a vengeance.'

In December 1831, nearly three years after William Burke had been hanged in Edinburgh's Lawnmarket, children playing near the Aberdeen Anatomical Theatre watched in horror as a dog, scraping the ground behind the theatre, hauled out and gnawed a mangled human limb. The alarm was raised, a crowd gathered, and other remains were found.

By now the crowd had become a mob. Francis Clerihew estimated that 10,000 people gathered in Hospital Row that afternoon. They broke into the theatre and chased the anatomist and his students from the building. Moir jumped through a window of his house and escaped through St Nicholas Churchyard.

After Moir and the students had gone, three bodies were found laid out for dissection. They were taken to Drum's Aisle in St Nicholas Church. Meanwhile, the mob smashed everything they could lay their hands on, even using a strong plank as a battering ram to undermine the walls and break them down. The building was ransacked and set on fire and when the Provost and a number of magistrates appeared on the scene and warned the rioters against their illegal actions they were ignored.

A party of soldiers was posted within the walls of Gordon's Hospital, near the Burkin' Hoose, but they did nothing to halt the destruction of the theatre. The fire engine arrived – too late. It made little difference, for there was no water to put out the fire.

'The work of demolition,' wrote Clerihew, 'was carried on and completed in a deliberate workman-like and substantial manner

St Nicholas Churchyard, where Andrew Moir obtained his bodies and where he was later buried.

by some forty or fifty active ruffians in the admiring presence of some 10 or 12,000 spectators and of an unresisting miliary and constabulary force'. Later, there were divided opinions on whether or not the police and military should have been used to halt the destruction of the theatre, particularly when there were fears that the mob would attack the Surgeon's Hall.

Three men were arrested and charged with setting fire to the theatre and assaulting Moir. One of the accused said he had gone to the theatre to see if he could find the body of another 'leddy in a box' – his grandmother, who had been interred a few weeks earlier. Each was jailed for twelve months.

Afterwards, argument raged over the way the authorities had dealt with the riot. Francis Clerihew, who was in his early twenties at the time and later became an interim Sheriff-Substitute, wrote in the *Aberdeen Magazine* about 'opposite opinions on the non-interference of the "terrors to evil-doers",' some blaming the police for making no attempt to prevent the destruction of private property, others saying that they had shown humanity by standing back and avoiding death and injury to the public.

Clerihew, who was known for his 'keen wit and pungent sarcasm', said that humanity in this case meant indecision. It allowed the rioters to make the plea at their trial that their actions were carried out under the eye of magistrates who were backed by a sufficient force to stop them, so that they had their implied sanction. He pointed out that the taxpayers would have to 'pay for this frolic of the mob and the magistracy'.

The Burkin' Hoose scandal was soon forgotten, but for Andrew Moir the shame of it lingered on. The macabre business of grave-robbing had come about because medical students were dissatisfied with the teaching of medicine in Aberdeen and frustrated by the lack of proper facilities for the study of anatomy. Moir, a gentle man, who did what he thought was his duty, became an object of contempt. In the eyes of many Aberdonians he was worse than Burke and Hare's patron, for Dr Knox had never gone out body-snatching and had given no encouragement to his students to rob graves.

The passing of the Anatomy Act in 1832 allowed him to work without fear of opposition, but the bitterness he felt at his treatment never left him. He contracted typhoid from a patient in 1844 and died at the early age of thirty-eight. His colleagues in the Aberdeen Medico-Chirurgical Society showed their respect for both the man and his work at his funeral. It started from the society's Medical Hall, whose Ionic portico dominates the south end of King Street, and ended in St Nicholas Churchyard.

Today, a large, crumbling stone marks his grave. He is said to have hidden from the howling mob under a tombstone in the town churchyard. He could never have foreseen that thirteen years later he would return to the kirkyard in his own coffin.

10
FLYTIN' O' THE WELLS

It was called the Flyting o' the Wells. It began one Saturday morning in the middle of the 19th century when the city's newspaper readers picked up their Aberdeen Herald and discovered that one of their drinking wells – the Well o' Spa – had 'gaun a' to crockanition'.* The well, facing neglect and decay, sent out a rhyming appeal to the public:

> Please, Aberdonians, ane an' a',
> To listen to the Well o' Spa,
> Wha wi' your leave wad humbly shaw
> A sma' petition;
> Now that I'm gaun, for guid an' a',
> To crockanition.

Behind that 'sma' petition' was William Anderson, a policeman-poet who had won a reputation for drawing portraits of local characters like Blin' Tibby Hogg, Feel Willie, Gley'd Sandy Gray and Moorican Roum. 'Flyting' was a Scots dialect word for scolding and was sometimes used to describe 'a contest in mutual abuse' between poets. Anderson, for instance, wrote about Tibby Hogg's flyting – 'She flyted at mornin', at noon an' at nicht, she flyted when wrang and she flyted when richt.'

The Well o' Spa, through Anderson's pen, complained that it was being 'neglected year by year'. It wondered why. Was its water less clear? Had its iron ore 'a' run oot'? It compared its own pure water with the 'muddy rill' in another well – 'my sister o' Firhill'.

In the following week's *Herald* the Firhill Well replied, with another local poet, William Cadenhead, taking its part:

> I'm sure the limpid Firhill Well
> (Excuse me thus to name mysel')
> Could mony a scandalous story tell
> 'Bout Well o' Spa,
> Wad gar her lugs ring like a bell
> To hear them a'.

*smithereens

But I forbear. In a' the toun
There's neither lad, nor lass, nor loun,
But my superior praise will soun,
My beauties tell –
I needna rin anither doun
To praise mysel'.

So on it went. The Well o' Spa said there were stories it had heard about the Firhill Well that would make an honest cheek turn pale, stories that would 'gar your lugs ring like a bell wi' perfect shame'. It hit out at the 'graceless crew' who hung about the Firhill well – 'rank unbelievers' on the Sabbath and souters and lazy weavers on a Monday.

The flyting took a new turn when the Corbie Well stepped in to halt this 'unseemly sough'. This latest outpouring of verse came from Cadenhead, who must have thought it time to put an end to the squabbling. He deplored the sneers at souters and weavers and the envy and taunts:

That's risen between the glaiket twa –
The Firhill and the Well o' Spa.

The wrangling ended and the wells, presumably cleaned up, went on with the business of supplying thirsty Aberdonians with their drinking water.

Of the three wells, the Spa was the best-known. It was famous in the Middle Ages for its curative chalybeate waters. George Jamesone, Scotland's first portrait painter, drank from it to cure an ailment of the bladder. It was moved to a new site in 1893 and again in 1977, when it was re-erected beside the Denburn Centre.

The Firhill Well, which dates from the mid-18th century, was better known as the Gibberie Wallie. The 'graceless crew' who hung about the well in Anderson's poem probably included the 'gibberie wifies' who sold gingerbread there on Sundays. In 1937 the well was moved from its site near Sunnybank Road to the St Machar Sports Ground in Sunnyside Road.

The Corbie Well, which stood on a wooded bank of the Denburn at Union Terrace, was moved to the Union Terrace Gardens. It was originally decorated with a number of civic relics – a lamp-post from the old Bow Brig, the weathercock from the former steeple of St Nicholas Church, and a bit of the famous bell 'Auld Lowrie'. All these have gone.

The Firhill Well – the 'Gibberie Wallie' – in St Machar's Sports Ground.

Today, the wells have been forgotten. They have been moved from their old sites and may one day become 'neglected year by year', just as they were in the old days. They have all dried up; not a drop of water spills from them. It may be, however, that another local poet – and there are plenty of fine Doric writers in Aberdeen – will come to their rescue and pour out some stirring lines that will save the old wells from once again going to crockanition.

The Firhill Well wasn't the only Gibberie Wallie in Aberdeen. There was another in Torry, on the south side of Greyhope Road, which was also known as John Lindsay's Well. Women sold gingerbread there on Saturday afternoons and on holidays. There was also a Corbie Well in Torry – and a Corbie Well Road, now called Mansefield Road.

There were no fewer than twenty-five wells in Torry, a number of them on the shore. Three were called St Fittick's, after the patron saint of the parish; these were sited at the Bay of Nigg, the salmon bothy, and beside the foghorn at Girdleness.

Near Greyhope Bay was the Bruntscallie or Craw Well, named after the Bruntscallie Rock, on which the *Oscar* was wrecked in April, 1813 (see Chapter 23). Jacob's Well was below the Torry Battery.

The Corbie Well in Union Terrace Gardens.

Forbes' Well was at North Kirkhill on Greyhope Road and the Pierhead or Icehouse Well was opposite the Pierhead.

The Pallen Well was at the back of a house at the Pierhead and another well of the same name at the back of a house at 161 Sinclair Road. The water from some of these Torry wells was said to be excellent – not like the 'muddy rill' of the Firhill Well, across the water in Aberdeen.

11
THE NEW MARKET

It was called the New Market. Built in 1842, it was the forerunner of the modern shopping mall, with everything under one roof. A huge arcade ran round the whole length of the building and a basement floor led into the Green. It was built to Archibald Simpson's design. His final triumphant touch was the magnificent main entrance on Market Street.

The New Market is still there today, having risen from the ashes of a devastating fire, survived radical changes, and had its name changed to the Aberdeen Market. But if events had taken a different turn it would now be the New Market railway station; with trains puffing in and out of it. Passengers would have stepped out of their carriages on to Union Street.

When railway mania broke out in the early 19th century, a new company called the Aberdeen Railway Company made plans to connect Aberdeen, Stonehaven and Laurencekirk with the already existing Arbroath and Forfar railway. The intention was to build a terminus at the angle of Guild Street and Market Street – and to take over the New Market buildings for the station.

The whole idea was scuppered when the New Market Company put their price on the deal – £50,000. The directors may have had in their minds the thought that they could scarcely sell out two years after holding a giant spree to mark the opening of the New Market, with thousands of people celebrating this momentous step into the city's future.

The townsfolk were agog at this new city landmark. On the afternoon of Friday 29 April, 1842, the opening day, the town had a half-holiday and the market was decorated with signs and banners. A banquet was organised (admission by payment) and between 2,000 and 3,000 people attended. Five long tables were laid out along the hall and two tiers of tables along the galleries.

There had never been anything quite like it. People promenaded round the shops and stalls for an hour, drinking in all the wonders of the New Market before sitting down to the banquet. After the opening, the first article sold was an 11 lb salmon, bought by the

The Aberdeen Market Building seen from the Green.

Lord Provost from David Robb's fishmonger's stall in the low market. That night, a spectacular display of fireworks brought an end to the celebrations.

Two years later, on April 29, 1882, which was exactly the fortieth anniversary of the opening, the dreams and hopes of the New Market planners literally turned to ashes. A few minutes before eight o'clock, fire broke out in a large stall in the upper west end of the building, tenanted by a Robert Ogg. He was a basket-maker and his highly inflammable goods were piled high from floor to ceiling. They proved a feeder for the blaze, which was made worse by the melting of gas pipes.

'The fire quickly ran along each gallery,' said one account, 'devouring toys, clothing, hardware, books and other commodities on sale in the various stalls, and almost simultaneously attacked the open pitch-pine roof, which, being dry as tinder, was speedily consumed. In about twenty minutes from the outbreak, part of the roof next the Green fell in, and in little over an hour the huge building was a seething cauldron of fire from end to end, only the stone walls remaining intact.'

The basement floor, or fish market, was fireproof and escaped the devastation. Men from the fire brigade, the military and the police fought the blaze, but it had taken too firm a hold before water could be turned on the flames. Some stall-holders and their assistants had hair-breadth escapes, leaping from windows or climbing down ladders. One elderly man, who had been helping a tenant, lost his life, suffocated by the smoke.

There were thirty-four butchers' stalls in the market-hall floor, while thirty traders had smaller stores in the gallery. Many tenants, under the impression that the building was fireproof, had failed to insure their stocks of goods. Some stall-holders got temporary premises in different parts of the city and a large wooden building was erected in the Green for the market-gardeners and fruit-sellers. A number of stalls were boarded off under the north and south galleries of the shattered building and were occupied by the butchers, while the butter and egg dealers displayed their wares in the front vestibule. The contracts for reconstruction were settled on May 27 and the building was immediately rebuilt almost in its original form.

Looking back on it thirty years later, one local chronicler said: 'The New Market has never regained its former glory.' Nevertheless, in the pre-war years it still retained some of its magic. I remember exploring its nooks and crannies when I was just a lad. The New Market odours still stay with me down the years, among them the smell of salty fish and raw meat (there seemed to be a remarkable number of butcher's shops), and the sweetly tantalising whiff of market candy.

The sharp Aberdeen tongue ('Fit like, min? Foo are ye?') mingled with the accents of Buchan and the Mearns, and from all over the hall a babel of voices floated up into the vast ceiling. The hall and basement provided food for the stomach, but upstairs was food for the mind. There was an Aladdin's Cave of second-hand books in the galleries, row upon row of them, piled high on stands that groaned under such intellectual weight: Greek and Latin classics, romances, adventure stories, books on law, architecture and mathematics – anything and everything a bookworm would want. There were other attractions, including getting your arm tattooed. For me, as a loon, the main attraction wasn't in the galleries, but downstairs in the long corridor leading from Union Street to the main hall. It was a slot machine which provided heart-stopping drama for a penny. When you put the penny in, the machine groaned and creaked into action to show a fireman rescuing a damsel from the first-floor window of a burning house. I often wondered what happened to it; it would be worth a fortune today.

Up in the galleries you could have your palm read by a fortune-teller. It didn't seem as if she could foretell what was to happen to the building that housed her, for in 1971 it became part of British Home Stores and was confined to two lower floors. An ugly gable-end at the east end of the Green told the world that it was now the Aberdeen Market. The *New* Market had gone for ever.

12
HAVE YOU HEARD THE ONE . . . ?

Have you heard the one about the American tourists who lost their way while travelling through Scotland? They finally came to the outskirts of a big city and the driver stopped the car and asked a boy the name of the town. 'I'll tell ye if ye gie me sixpence,' said the youngster. 'Drive on!' said the American, 'I guess this is Aberdeen.'

Aberdeen got its reputation for meanness from stories like that. Between the wars, it would have raised hoots of laughter; today, not even a smirk. The fact is that the mean Aberdonian story is rarely, if ever, heard. It is almost as extinct as the Dodo.

Aberdonians have always been the first to laugh at such stories. It has even been said that they were the people who thought them up. Back in 1925, Allan Junior, compiler of *Canny Tales fae Aberdeen*, claimed that there was a secret club in the city whose members met to manufacture tight-fisted tales about their fellow citizens.

His book contained two views of Aberdeen. One showed Union Street completely deserted – it was a flag day. In the second picture the street was packed with people. That was Aberdeen on a house-to-house collection day.

But the hard-headed folk of the Granite City knew how to deal with such slanders. They always settled an argument over a drink, keeping in mind an old Aberdeen proverb that said, 'If ony man insults ye by offerin' ye a drink – swallow the insult.'

There was a scattering of crisp one-liners in Allan Junior's book. One was about an Aberdonian who gave a waiter a tip, but the horse didn't run, and another was about an Aberdonian who kept his mouth open in cold weather because there was a nip in the air.

Harry Gordon, the Laird of Inversnecky, cashed in on the 'mean Aberdonian' vogue despite the fact that he was an Aberdonian himself. He said that Aberdeen motorists took every corner on two wheels to save wear on the tyres, that they were fond of rubber because it gave, and that an Aberdonian never finished his soup because he hated to tip the plate. Here are three stories from Inversnecky:

Little Willie – 'Hey, faither, let's go tae the Centennial Pageant, it's only a shillin.'

Aberdeen on a flag day . . .

Father – 'Next time, laddie, next time.'

Wife – 'Have ye seen ma thimble, Angus?'
Angus – 'Aye. Ye'll find it beside the whisky bottle. I gave
MacWhister a nicht cap last nicht.'

A visitor was nosing round the only second-hand bookshop in
Inversnecky. Picking up a well-worn volume he asked the
shopkeeper, 'Is this a free translation'.
'Na,' replied the shopkeeper, 'it'll cost ye 7/6'.

Of course, the success of such stories depended on how they were
told. Aberdeen had two outstanding storytellers – Sir James Taggart,
who was Lord Provost of the city from 1914 to 1919; and the first
Marquis of Aberdeen and Temair. On a number of occasions the
two raconteurs appeared together on public platforms to compete
for the title of Prince of Storytellers, and inevitably the old 'mean
Aberdonian' myth figured largely in their repertoire. Typical of the
quickfire Taggart quip was the story about the Aberdonian who went
off on a month's holiday with a dark green shirt and a pound note
and changed neither of them!

Whenever the opportunity arose they tilted at each other. Taggart
once told how Lord Aberdeen had been walking along Edinburgh's

. . . and on a house-to-house collection day.

High Street when a drunk man collided with him. A policeman reproved the man, saying: 'Do you know you have run into the Marquis of Aberdeen and Temair?' 'Good Lord!' said the man, 'am I as bad as that? Wis there twa o' them?'

Sir James brought Lord Aberdeen's name into his anecdotes as often as he could. One of them was about a farmer who, having bought a farm from Lord Aberdeen, travelled into the city. In Union Street he boarded a tramcar and asked what the fare was to Mannofield. 'Twopence,' replied the conductor. 'And how much for the loonie?' 'Oh, we winna charge anything for him.' 'Ah, weel,' said the farmer. 'Let the loonie aff at Mannofield and I'll walk.'

Lord Aberdeen was probably thinking of Lord Provost Taggart when he related the story of a tourist who was told by a railway porter that Kintore was a royal burgh. 'Have you a Provost and Magistrates?' asked the tourist. 'Ay, surely,' said the porter. 'And does your Provost go about with a chain?' 'Na!' said the porter. 'He jist gangs aboot loose.'

His Lordship's stories were usually drawn-out affairs, but he occasionally told a 'quickie'. There was, for instance, the one about the tramp who tried to beg money from an Aberdonian. 'I've seen better days, sir,' he said. 'So have I,' replied the Aberdonian, 'but I havna time to discuss the weather the noo.'

Peter Esslemont, a well-known Aberdeen businessman, produced two small booklets, entitled *Stories Frae Aberdeen,* which carried 'epigrams, conundrums, quotations and jokes'. Some of the jokes had the usual 'mean' streak about them, like the one about an Aberdonian who met a friend he hadn't seen for twenty years. 'Remember, Jock,' he said, 'it's your turn to stan' yer hand.'

For a time before the war Aberdeen was hit by a wave of Jewish jokes. Allan Junior's collection included a section entitled 'The Aberdeen Jew'. In his foreword he denied a suggestion that there were no Jews in the Granite City. 'There is one,' he wrote. 'He cannot raise enough money to get out of the city. His name is Isaac Levi. For some time he called himself Donald MacSporran and wore a kilt.'

Isaac featured in a long string of Jewish jokes. Some were on the lines of the old 'vant to buy a vatch' theme, and a number were used to perpetuate the 'mean Aberdonian' myth. One was called 'Getting the better of an Aberdonian'. It described how Sandy Gordon prided himself that no one had ever got the better of him in a financial transaction. 'Sandy,' said Isaac, 'I will sell you something which cost me three pence for two pence.' Sandy bought it. It was a 3d tram ticket.

A number of the jokes played off the 'grippy' Aberdonian against the tightfisted Jew. 'It is on record', it was said, 'that Isaac once went into partnership with an Aberdonian, but they had to dissolve it at the end of a week. Neither of them could sleep for watching the other.'

The Aberdeen Jewish jokes were innocent enough, but the war put an end to such humour; not even Isaac, who had a strong streak of Granite City blood running through his veins, was allowed to continue. For different reasons, the 'mean Aberdonian' story also disappeared. In post-war years it seemed to have little place in a city that had become the oil capital of Europe.

In 1989, it looked as if the 'mean Aberdonian' joke was making a comeback when Aberdeen journalist Ted Kidd produced *Tell it to an Aberdonian!*, a book about the wit and humour of the North-east. While the city's meanness sneaked into one or two pages, the book generally covered a broader field of humour. In it, Ted mentioned another town that carried the 'meanest city' tag – Gabrovo in Bulgaria.

So the mean Aberdonian seems to have been banished for good. There are no more moths flying out of tightly-closed sporrans, no more Aberdeen proverbs like 'Never be the first to say "What's yours?"', no more tramps asking for a copper and being told 'D'ye ken far ye are, man, this is Aiberdeen'. The last word should probably be left to Harry Lauder, who once said that the 'Scotch' joke was 'a lie we have never taken the trouble to kill because it has been fine *free* publicity for us as a nation'.

By the way, have you heard the one about the Aberdonian who went to his doctor with a complaint and was told to give up drink. The patient was walking out of the surgery when the doctor reminded him that there was a five guinea fee for his advice. 'Aye,' replied the man, 'but I'm nae takin' it.'

13
THE BATTLE OF CASTLEHILL

Aberdeen had a military barracks on Castlehill for almost a century and a half. It was built in 1794 and occupied by the military until 1935. For the next thirty years it was used as a lodging house. It became a slum, a place to be avoided by respectable citizens, and in 1965 it was demolished. Today, multi-storey municipal tower blocks stand on the site.

The only 'battle' ever fought at Castlehill took place in June 1802, when a regiment of Ross and Cromarty Rangers, who were garrisoned there, found themselves besieged in the barracks – by the townsfolk. It happened on the birthday of George III. The garrison commander and a number of officers had been invited to the Town House by the civic authorities to drink his Majesty's health. The wine flowed freely, paid for out of the Common Good Fund, and some of the officers became intoxicated.

When they returned to the barracks a group of lads in the Castlegate were having a friendly 'battle' – throwing squibs, dirt and garbage at each other. The youngsters, seeing that the officers were 'under the influence', stopped their own game and started chucking the garbage at the commander and his men.

The officers, their decision-making muddled by too much wine, called out the regiment from the barracks without the authority or presence of a civil magistrate. 'The consequence of this,' wrote William Kennedy in his *Annals of Aberdeen*, 'was that in a very short time a tumult and disorder ensured, and the populace and the military became exasperated at each other. The soldiers, set free from discipline and unrestrained by their officers, repeatedly fired with ball cartridge upon the people assembled in the Castlegate, four of whom were unfortunately killed, and many severely wounded.'

Kennedy's description of what he called this 'atrocious act' captured little of the real drama of the Battle of Castlehill. A much more vivid account appeared in the *Aberdeen Journal*, reporting on an anniversary day that began 'with the usual marks of joy'. The Ross and Cromarty Rangers began firing their muskets long before garbage was thrown at them. They fired three volleys in the barrack yard at

The Castlegate, scene of the Batlle of Castlehill.

twelve o'clock to mark the king's birthday, and when the magistrates and VIPs drunk his Majesty's health in the Town Hall, a detachment of the rangers fired off repeated volleys on the Plainstanes. ('The Plainstanes' was a nickname given to the Castlegate after a spacious raised pavement was laid out in the centre of the square. Here, the town's top people 'passed an hour or two in walking before dinner, bracing their nerves in the free air and discussing the politics of the day.')

There was plenty to discuss that day, for the rangers turned their guns on the townsfolk. 'They ran upon the people in the street with their arms in their hands,' reported the *Journal*, 'and began firing upon them with ball, indiscriminately and in every direction, and some were even seen taking deliberate aim at individuals.

'Many of the bullets went through windows and doors in the west end of Castle Street and in the head of the Shiprow and narrow Wynd, and others were found at a greater distance through the town.'

A local man, who was a private in the rifle corps, which was recruiting in the city at the time, was standing at the corner of the Plainstones and was shot through the head. He died on the spot. Thomas Milne, a mason, John Moir, a young boy and the only son of a widow, and William Gibb, a barber's apprentice, were all wounded and died next day. Ten other people were wounded.

The provost and magistrates appeared and ordered the Rangers back into the barracks. They also ordered a mounted guard of armed citizens outside the barracks, fearful that the angry townsfolk would take some action that 'might have led to further fatal consequences'.

The soldiers were confined to barracks until the following week. Then, about one o'clock on Tuesday morning, the regiment 'marched out of town in dead silence and without the beat of drum by the way of the Broadhill and Old-town Links on their way northwards'. It was said that every soldier was in his stocking soles to deaden the sound of their departure.

That wasn't the end of the story. Many of Aberdeen's principal citizens decided to press for a prosecution in the names of the parents of those who had been killed. The result was that three officers and two sergeants, who were said to be largely responsible, were brought to trial in the High Court in Edinburgh on 6 July 1803. The jury found two of the officers not guilty. The third officer absconded on the day of the trial and was outlawed for non-appearance. The verdict on the two sergeants was 'not proven'.

The fury of the Aberdeen people involved in the prosecution can well be imagined. It was made worse by the fact that they were left with enormous expenses to lawyers, agents and their retainers in Edinburgh. The cost was £600, plus the personal charges of many of the witnesses. But the total sum was far short of the money raised by voluntary subscription.

14
THE CASTLE SPECTRE

Down at the bottom of Mackie Place, a lane that branches off Skene Street, the dark waters of the Denburn run through a corner of Aberdeen that few people know. Shadowed by trees, cut off from the rush of traffic above, it seems an eerie place. Back in the middle of the 19th century a gaunt, five-storeyed building stood there. It was known as the Haunted House, for ghosts were seen around it, white wraiths floating out of the blackness. Fiery eyes stared out from hedges and an unearthly squawling of cats was heard. It was a place that people avoided . . .

The Haunted House was said to strike fear into the hearts of nervous passers-by. Standing in its own grounds, it overlooked the Denburn in an area immediately to the west of Mackie Place known as the Galleries, almost opposite Whitehouse Street. The name 'Galleries' is said to come from old Celtic words meaning the hollow of the flowing water – the Denburn. The real name of the Haunted House was the White House, as in the street, but because of its unusual architecture some people nicknamed it the Castle.

To get some idea of how the Castle looked you have to go down Mackie Place, cross the small bridge over the Denburn, and go through a gateway to where an imposing mansion with twin ogee-shaped front gables can be seen. This striking building, a contemporary of the White House, dates from the late 18th century and was one of Aberdeen's earliest granite houses. It is semi-detached, with curving flights of steps leading to two central doors.

In its early days it stood in a picturesque setting, but now huge tenements rise around it. The twin houses are marked Nos. 4 and 5 Mackie Place, but there was also a No. 6 – the White House. Unlike Nos. 4 and 5, which survived the years, No. 6 disappeared from the scene in the early years of this century.

Its owner was Alexander D. Forbes, an eccentric character who retired to Aberdeen after spending many years in the East. He was half-brother to Dr John Forbes, Professor of Hebrew at Aberdeen University. In October, 1876, he launched a new magazine which, because it was printed and distributed from the Haunted House,

The Galleries today. The White House, No. 6, was demolished.

was named the *Castle Spectre*. 'We are wont to look across the Atlantic for novelties in journalism,' commented a writer in *Scottish Notes and Queries*, 'but we have to look no further than our own town for as unique a novelty as ever appeared. It is irreproachable from a typographical point of view, while the startling frankness and originality of many of its articles come as a surprise to jaded journal readers.'

The woodcuts in the earlier numbers, including a cover sketch of the Castle, were done by the eldest daughter of John Hill Burton, the historian.

Was the White House really haunted? Did ghosts really float about the banks of the Denburn? In January 1888 a correspondent, C.S.L., wrote to *Scottish Notes and Queries* saying he had heard of the haunted house in Mackie Place and had made some inquiries. They had produced no results, 'except that some years ago a student was found dead at the garden wall'. The following month, another correspondent, J.M.B. (J. Malcolm Bulloch, the historian) contacted *Scottish Notes and Queries* suggesting that 'Mr Forbes, of the real *Castle Spectre*, might be able to set us right about its traditional ghostly ancestor'.

In fact, Mr Forbes had set the public right twelve years earlier in the first issue of the *Castle Spectre*. Only 100 copies of it were printed, and these were quickly sold out. A reprint was published later, but it is more than likely that many people missed it and never read the revelations about the Haunted House. Those who did discovered that there were down-to-earth explanations for the ghostly figures, the peering eyes and the caterwauling. This is what Alex Forbes had to say about it:

> We are the dwellers in that house in the neighbourhood of Skene Street known to the oldest inhabitants as the Haunted House, to younger inhabitants as the Castle, and to the Post Office as No. 6 Mackie Place. In former days we were 'desp'rate wicked'. We dressed ourselves in white sheets and popped out upon passers-by, frightening them into fits. We used to scoop out the largest turnips (which we always stole) and, having cut out slices to represent eyes, nose and mouth, light candles in them and stick them on poles in hedges, just where they would suddenly glimmer out upon the greatest possible number of women and children.

> We used to lie behind low walls and growl like bears, or howl like dogs, or caterwaul like cats whenever any weakly-looking person was passing. We were very careful not to play our tricks upon strong-looking men – or women either for that matter – for fear of being found out and getting a thrashing. In short, we were the terror of the neighbourhood.

Forbes went on to say that a change had come over the spirit of the times.

> People were beginning – only beginning however – to disbelieve in white sheets, illuminated turnips, table-turning, spirits writing on slates, spirits taken internally, etc. Spirits, unless they alter their habits, are likely to fall into complete disrepute.

They had once been the terror of the district; now, with the publication of the Castle Spectre, they were to become its delight.

> Our periodical appearance will be hailed by millions with indescribable emotions of joy.

The imprint on the first issue of the *Castle Spectre* said it was printed and published by A. D. Forbes, 6 Mackie Place, Aberdeen; the second number was by 'the Mackie Place Co'., and in the third issue it had changed to 'The Galleries (late Mackie Place) Co., Galleries, Aberdeen. It appeared monthly and carried a sketch of the Castle on the title page.

Its contents ranged over religion, poetry, politics, and fiction; it launched what was described as 'a sensational novel entitled *The Grahams' First Governness'*. One of the poems in the first issue was 'To Grannie on her seventy-sixth birthday':

> Words cannot tell thee of our love;
> What they can not express
> Let this convey – the firstling of
> Our Muse, and our new Press.

Forbes also had a profitable little sideline – 'Jam-pot Labels, printed by A. D. Forbes'. He advertised them in the *Spectre*, alongside an offer of 'Indian Tea, just arrived, direct from the Grower, a parcel of finest Assam Pekoe Souchong'. In the July issue in 1879 the magazine carried a reminder to its readers – 'Memo for July – Good housewives will even yet, so late is the season, order Jam-pot Labels'.

One of Alex Forbes' helpers was Katherine Trail, whose father was Professor William Milligan, of the Chair of Biblical Criticism at King's College. In her book, *Reminiscences of Old Aberdeen*, she wrote about Forbes and 'the very strange old house known as The Castle', which she said was a hospitable house to her and 'many other young friends'. It was their interest in writing that resulted in Forbes' plan to start a magazine.

'To help us,' she wrote, 'he bought a printing machine, which was installed in the dining-room and took up a large part of the room. He printed our effusions and published them every month under the title of "The Castle Spectre". I am afraid our enthusiasm waned long before that of the editor and in the latter years of the magazine's existence Mr Forbes was practically the sole contributor.'

The issue of October, 1888, No. 145, carried an article entitled 'The Vanishing of the Spectre'. It announced the closing of the magazine – 'the last emanation, or exhalation, from the banks of the Denburn', wrote Forbes. He pointed out that, apart from a few paragraphs that had been set up in the earlier numbers by the junior Spectres, every piece of type in its 608 pages had been set up 'by the Spectre himself'. His final article gave some intriguing background information, not least being the fact that his helpers ages ranged from twelve to eighteen.

> There were forty female writers, ten male and eight anonymous, of whom four appeared to be male and four female. The ladies supplied us with ninety four stories, four letters, nine descriptive pieces, and thirty-seven

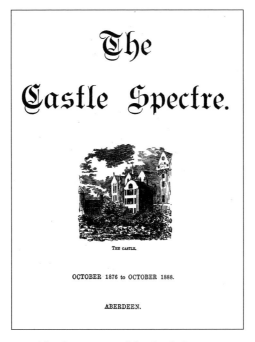

The front cover of the *Castle Spectre*.

poetical. We accepted from the gentlemen thirteen stories, one letter, three descriptive pieces, and six poetical. Of articles sent us we rejected wonderfully few.

Forbes, according to Katherine Trail, was 'a very curious man'. He had a family of four, two sons and two daughters, and was 'most hospitable and kind to all their friends'. But the death of his wife changed him. He swore that he would never again go outside his door. It was a vow he kept for many years, but it changed his character. He let his hair grow long – in the end it was down to his waist – and to the outside world it seemed as if a real Spectre lived in the gloomy Haunted House in the Galleries.

The Castle was demolished in the 1920s. There were no more glittering eyes in the dark, no more howling dogs and caterwauling cats, no more white sheets and 'desp'rate wicked' ghosts. *Tempora mutantur, nos et mutamur in illis,* as the Spectre said.*

---

*The times are perpetually changing, and we with the times.

15
SPLIT-THE-WIN'

Where Causewayend and lang George Street
Join hands upon the Northern Way,
Through winter wild and summer sweet
Stood Split-the-Win' for many a day.

When that poem was written in the early years of the 20th century it ended with a line saying that Split-the-Win' had become 'just the whisper of a passing name'. This was partly true, but, in fact, the name has lingered on over the years. It has been used by succeeding generations of Aberdonians to describe a corner of the town where the main north road sweeps down from Kittybrewster to Calsayseat Road and 'splits' into George Street and Powis Place.

The original Split-the-Win' was a small triangular piece of ground with two buildings on it, one of them an inn. In those days there was no Powis Place or Powis Terrace and the northern limit of the houses was where Causewayend (St Stephen's) United Free Church was built in 1879. In George Street there was only one house north of Fraser Place on the east side and a few scattered houses on the west side.

So Split-the-Win' was isolated from the city, surrounded by fields, bleaching greens and pasture land, with the Aberdeenshire Canal running sluggishly on its way a few yards to the east. There was a nursery with an entrance made from whale's jawbones and white and yellow gowans carpeted a field known to children as 'the Gowany Park'. There was a Gowan Brae on what is now Fraser Place.

The inn was called 'Splittie's', but it was so narrow and gloomy that it was also nicknamed 'The Coffin'. William Smith, who wrote about Split-the-Win' in the *Book of Powis* in 1906, said that the pub was 'a mere bandbox of a building'. Nevertheless, going to Splittie's for a 'bitter' on a Sunday was 'a popular pilgrimage' and 'See ye at Split-the-Win'' was as familiar a phrase as 'See ye at the Queen' or 'See ye at the Monkeyhouse' in later years.

Oddly enough, the corner house at Causewayend and Canal Road was also called the 'Coffinie' in the middle of the 19th century. The bridge that carried Canal Road over the railway was known as the

Tarry Brig and people living today still remember Isy Mason's farm, which you looked down on from the bridge. Beside the 'Coffinie' was a menagerie run by old Peter Kerkless (Hercules). 'It was a veritable Noah's Ark,' wrote Smith, 'and contained all manner of animals and creeping things . . . mice, rats, cats, dogs, ferrets, squirrles, hawks, larks and so on in ascending scale of importance and magnitude till the tame, but chained fox was reached. For a brief period the menagerie gloried in the possession of a mangy wolf.'

The most curious creature mentioned by Smith was 'a wild untamed goloch'. A goloch is an earwig, better known in this part of the country as a forky-tail, but the mind boggles at how anyone could even contemplate taming such an insect. Peter's corner, like Split-the-Win', has long since disappeared.

Splittie's had one gable facing George Street, the other Causewayend (Powis Place), and the house next to it was Calsayseat, owned by the Leslies of Powis. It was rented out to William Souttar, the father of James Souttar, the architect, and Robinson Souttar, MP for Dumfries. In 1908, Robinson Souttar wrote to the *Aberdeen Daily Journal* about an article he had seen in the paper on Split-the-Win'.

'Where do you think I last heard that name?' he wrote. 'In Rome, of all places in the world! I was introduced to Monsignor Fraser, one of the most influential men at the Vatican. He said, "Are ye Scotch?" "Ay," I said. "Are ye?" "Surely man," he said. "I'm fae Aberdeen." So am I," I said . . . "Whaur did ye live?" says he. "Calsayseat," says I. "Split-the-Win'!" says he. "Man, I lived there mysel'." "Surely," he added, "ye're nae a son of William Souttar?" When I assured him that I was, he said, "My father knew him well."'

There was a pump in the garden of Calsayseat and the landlady at 'Splittie's' thought that the cold spring water from it mixed fine with her whisky. Mrs Souttar allowed her to take it because she felt that the more water the whisky contained the better it would be for the drinkers.

Before the railway came, strings of carriers' carts came down from Kittybrewster, stopping at Splittie's so that the drivers could get a drink. Their ale was accompanied by 'great whangs of bread and cheese'. Most of the carriers were cottars; 'honest, capable, and reliable to a degree,' said Smith, although they were often quick to take the law into their own hands. The Kemnay carrier, an old worthy in home-spun hodden grey, was a familiar figure, as was the blind bellman from Kinellar, who carried goods to Kinellar from Aberdeen.

Split-the-Win'.

Famous coaches rattled past Split-the-Win', among them the 'Defiance' on its way from Edinburgh to Inverness. The red and gold Royal Mail coaches, with the lion and unicorn on their panels, clattered up Causewayend, their drivers and guards resplendent in tall hats and bright red coats. The 'Banks of Don' passed Split-the-Win' in the morning and returned at night and the 'Earl of Fife' could be seen coming and going from Banff.

'Splittie's' landlady was popular because of her whisky, cooled by the Calsayseat water, but if William Cadenhead is to be believed she must have had competition from the legendary Kitty Brewster, who 'sellt a dram' on the road to Hilton. Cadenhead, in his poem 'Kitty Brewster', wrote:

> Her dram was good, but O, her ale,
> 'Twas it that did her credit.

Did Kitty Brewster really exist? It seems that she didn't. G.M. Fraser, in his *Aberdeen Street Names,* quoted a 1754 act about road repairs between the town 'and Katy Browster's Feu on the Hilton Road'. That seemed to suggest that there had been a real Kitty Brewster, but the name went even farther back. Reference was made in records of 1673 to 'ane merch stone in the Den called Kettiebrauster'.

Cadenhead regretted the changes in the area – 'Kitty's canty but-and-ben,' he said, had been 'levelled with the divot.' Robert Anderson, author of *Aberdeen in Bygone Days*, who said he was 'an old Causewayend loon', felt the same about the disappearance of Split-the-Win'. 'The lines of Causewayend and George Street at Split-the-Win',' he wrote, 'have completely lost the attraction and the charm they once possessed.' When the Powis estate feued out the parks and fields in the area for housing in the 1880s, Calsayseat and Split-the-Win' were 'doomed to extinction'. The Leslies of Powis gifted the site to the Church of Scotland, who were planning a new kirk at Kittybrewster. It opened in 1895.

Anderson, the Causewayend loon, would have been even more unhappy if he could have seen Split-the-Win' today. Traffic roars past it on a busy dual carriageway, and the kirk that took the place of 'Splittie's', with its flight of steps and pillared doorway facing north, ended up with a 'For Sale' sign under its high-pitched north gable.

Split-the-Win' . . . it is a wonderfully evocative name. A name from nowhere, for nobody knows who first called it that, or when. Robert Anderson thought it highly expressive; thoroughly redolent of the dialect, he said, conveying its meaning instantly. Stand there on a winter's day, with a bitter wind blowing down from Kittybrewster, and you can almost *feel* it splitting into two, one half bouncing off down George Street, the other half howling away to Causewayend.

16
MAN DOWN A LUM

This is the story of the great Chimney Pot mystery – the tale of a man who fell down a lum. Not a big factory chimney, just an ordinary household lum. It happened back in the 19th century, in the early fifties, and it was described as a 'thrilling incident'.

The setting was a sordid corner of the city around the Castlegate. It was the haunt of beggars and prostitutes. Mason's Court was entirely occupied by prostitutes. Beggars with sore arms and legs lay about the streets forming 'a disgusting sight'. Families couldn't send their servants out without having them bombarded with indecent and blasphemous language.

There was no street worse than Sinclair's Close, which ran from Justice Street towards the Castlehill Barracks, and it was in this area that the drama took place. It began when a man was seen to climb out of the attic window of a house in Justice Street. He staggered along the roof and then tumbled into the street. Horrified onlookers thought he must be dead, or certainly badly injured, and people ran to the spot to help him. He was nowhere to be seen.

It was dark and they searched all round the houses. There was a certain air of disbelief among the searchers, almost as if they couldn't believe their own eyes. 'People ran hither and thither and for some time could make nothing of the affair,' wrote a local scribe, William Skene. Then some searchers heard low groans, but when they tried to trace them there was still no sign of the fallen man.

They went into a woodyard at the back of a house known as the Howff. Still no sign – the body had vanished. Finally, someone said that the groans seemed to be coming from a chimney in Sinclair's Close. It didn't seem possible, but they sent for an old residenter called Robbie Masson, a joiner, whose workshop was in Sinclair's Close. He was also a funeral director, so he was ready for any eventuality. Within minutes, he reported back that there *was* a man inside the chimney – and he was firmly imbedded there.

The only way to get him out was by the fireplace – and the fireplace was less than 18 inches high. Undaunted, Robbie and his helpers sent for picks and set to work taking out the bricks. In a

Houses in the Sinclair Close area of the Castlegate. Note the broken chimneys.

short time, the mysterious man in the lum was helped out of the fireplace, more dead than alive, covered with soot from head to foot. He was taken away to the police office. It turned out that he had been drinking with a number of people in the attic, which entered from Mussel Close.

'There had been a good deal of liquor going,' wrote William Skene, 'some quarrelling occurred, and in a wooden dream the young man, not knowing what he was about, clambered out by the skylight and on to the roof. He ran along the ridges until he came to the end and as the chimney tops were levelled down to the roof, when he came to the end, instead of dropping off the housetop, he dropped miraculously down the chimney feet first. Had he missed going down the chimney-hole he would have been dashed to pieces.'

So that was that. But there were still questions to answer. How on earth could a man fall down a chimney pot? He wasn't Santa Claus. It wasn't like the old days when chimney sweeps sent youngsters up the lums to clean them. It seemed impossible.

Old sketches of the area show the chimneys to be very ordinary, with scarcely enough room for a cat to get down, let alone a man, but in the more decrepit streets there were broken lums and no lums at all. In some chimneys the stonework below the pot was crumbling away, leaving a great hole where the chimney pot had been. Skene made no mention of this and gave no indication of the size of the chimney. All that he said was that it was 'a most remarkable escape from sudden death'.

At any rate, it proved that Santa Claus wasn't the only man who could drop down a chimney and come out unscathed.

17
A RAT IN THE CHAPEL

A rat can be seen skulking against a wall in St Mary's Chapel at St Nicholas Church, Aberdeen. The story of how it got there is a horrifying one – a tale that should serve as a warning to people with itchy fingers and lying tongues.

It all began centuries ago when a bishop planted three apple trees near the Nethergate Wall at the Chapel. The trees flourished, producing fine crops, but one day the bishop found that all the apples had been stolen and branches of the trees had been broken. He was furious. He thought the thief should suffer 'the torment of hell' and cursed him 'with candle, book and bell'.

> May he lack when alive
> Both of water and bread
> And conscience torment him
> Until he is dead.
>
> May his flesh and his sinews
> Be torn from his bones
> By rats and may none
> Hear his last dying groans.

One of the friars, Friar David, told the bishop that he had had a dream in which he saw the lad who had stolen the apples. He was a choirboy named Gregory Law. The bishop summoned Gregory, had him flogged, then imprisoned him in the vault for three days without food. When they went to release him on the fourth day he was dead. Only a skeleton was left – the rats had eaten his flesh.

Later, Friar David confessed that *he* had stolen the apples, not Gregory. He told the bishop that since Gregory's death he could find no peace or rest. The bishop listened to his confession, decided to forgive him, and removed the curse, but next day the friar was also found dead – and the rats had eaten *his* flesh.

> The Bishop to prove
> He the Friar did assoil,
> Placed a rat made of stone
> On St Mary's aisle.

The stone rat is still there today, but whether or not the bishop was buried in the old kirkyard no one knows. He might well have been, for over the centuries many tombstones have been removed or broken up. John Montgomerie, the mason who made Aberdeen's famous Mercat Cross, was buried there, but all traces of his grave have vanished.

The tombstones that remain have their own stories, some sad, some funny – some just plain curious. The old kirkyard has become to Aberdeen what Père-Lachaise is to Paris. Hundreds of people flock to the French cemetery to see where the rich and famous are buried. It is as popular a tourist attraction as the Champs Elysées, even providing visitors with an official guide book.

In Aberdeen, St Nicholas kirkyard hasn't quite reached such heights, although a guide book was issued some years ago, but in summer it is a favourite haunt of city shoppers and office workers, who use the venerable stones as back-rests when they eat their lunchtime snacks. Not all the picnickers know that they are sitting on a slice of the city's history.

Row after row of tombstones stand, or lie, like pieces of a jigsaw puzzle. Fit them together and they add up to a picture of Aberdeen going back to the 16th century . . . a roll-call of the provosts, lawyers, clergymen, doctors, architects, artists and writers who brought renown to the Granite City.

Behind the faded lettering on the stones lie some odd tales. For instance, a large, ornate stone marks the grave of William Cruden, Provost of Aberdeen from 1784 to 1785, who was well-known for the inordinate pride he took in being a provost. Even when his wife died, she was buried in a fashion befitting the spouse of a provost of the city – bells were tolled and guns were fired on the Castlehill.

When the provost was on a visit to London a fellow-Aberdonian played a practical joke on him by pinning a placard on his back with the words, 'I am Provost Cruden of Aberdeen'. As he walked through the streets, stranger after stranger greeted him warmly by his name. The unsuspecting provost was delighted that his fame had spread so far south.

Provost Cruden was born in Strichen, but he seems to have adopted the habits of a canny Aberdonian. On one occasion he was folding his clothes in front of a friend when a potato fell out of his coat pocket. The provost explained that because of the price and scarcity of vegetables he always told his daughter to put a potato in any spare corner of his clothing.

There are a number of provosts buried in the St Nicholas kirkyard, but not all were as popular as William Cruden. Alexander Gordon, who was provost from 1668 to 1689, became involved in a row over Episcopalian and Presbyterian forms of worship. The Presbyterians, according to one report, took the provost, 'put a cape about his neck, led him about the town and afterwards caused him to hang two dogs, one of which he called Presbyter and the other Quaker'. The provost was then shut up in prison.

Robert Cruickshank, from Banchory, who was Provost of Aberdeen from 1693 to 1696, is also buried at St Nicholas. He was low in the popularity stakes because he always wanted his own way. He was also a man of considerable vanity. When the Ruthrieston pack horse bridge was being rebuilt by the River Dee, near the Bridge of Dee, Provost Cruickshank had his arms carved on a stone which was built into the pack bridge.

The Council, upset at not being consulted about it, had the stone removed and offered it back to the provost – at a price. Cruickshank refused. Later, the Council replaced the stone on the bridge but put it where nobody could see it. By 1705, however, people seemed to have become resigned to their opinionated civic leader. The stone with the provost's arms was put back the right way round and information added saying that he was provost when the bridge was built. The stone can still be seen on the bridge.

When Cruickshank stepped down from the Council he tried to put his son-in-law, John Johnson, forward as a candidate. The opposition stayed away on election day and there was no quorum, but Cruickshank brought people off the streets and managed to get Johnson elected. There was such a row over the matter that Johnson had to stand down and a new election was held. All this fighting and fussing didn't seem to affect the stubborn provost. He died in 1717 at the ripe old age of ninety-four.

Granite tombstones rise above the graves of the men who built the Granite City. Archibald Simpson, the architect whose designs gave it the Granite City tag, died a bachelor in 1847 and was laid to rest in the shadow of the 'Mither Kirk'. John Smith, Aberdeen's first city architect, who was known as 'Tudor Johnnie' because his designs were in the Elizabethan style, is also buried there. He designed the North Church (now the Arts Centre) in King Street and the Grecian screening in front of St Nicholas Church. His father, William Smith, built the houses on the west side of Marischal Street and was known as 'Sink 'em Smith'.

Aberdeen might never have become the Granite City if it hadn't been for the foresight of a civil engineer called John Gibb. The Town Council, who owned Rubislaw Quarry, put it up for sale after being told that the stone in it was 'of poor quality and no use for building'. Gibb didn't believe this assessment. He stepped in and bought it for a mere £13. When he died he was buried between John Ross, who was Chief Constable of Aberdeenshire for thirty years, and William Cruden, the provost with the potatoes in his pockets.

John Ramsay, the Aberdeen poet, knew well in advance where his last resting place would be. Nearly forty years before he died and was buried at St Nicholas, Ramsay wrote about what he called his 'secret place of rest' in a poem entitled 'My Grave'. Printed in the *Aberdeen Herald* in January 1833, under the name Sigma, it was said to be 'oft-quoted'. Ramsay didn't want too many people peering at his grave, but he worried that some might stay away because of its 'uninviting gloom'.

> . . . as if there seemed to hover near
> In fancy's ken, a thing of fear,
> And viewed with superstitious awe
> Be duly shunned and scarcely draw
> The sidelong glance of passer-by,
> As haunt of sprite with blasting eye.

As a boy, Ramsay was fascinated by the St Nicholas Church bells – the bells of St Lawrence and St Mary. He learned all he could about campanology and soon became a competent bell-ringer. Also buried at St Nicholas is Lachlan Mackinnon, author of *Recollections of an Old Lawyer*, who recalled seeing the burning of the East Church and the ancient spire of St Nicholas in 1874, four years after John Ramsay's death. He was allowed into the churchyard by a police officer, Inspector Dey, whose size earned him the nickname of 'the longest Dey'.

Mackinnon described how he 'saw the flames enwrapping the wooden spire and the lead running down it in molten streams, observed the clock hands drop to the bottom of the dial, heard the fall of Auld Lowrie, the historic bell, as it crashed to the bottom of the tower, and witnessed the collapse of the spire as it bowed towards the east and came plunging down in a cascade of fire'.

Auld Lowrie (the St Lawrence bell) hung in the St Nicholas steeple for over 500 years. It was gifted to the church in 1351 along with the

St Mary bell. When the present granite steeple was built a carillon of thirty-seven new bells was installed. Today, there are forty-eight bells ringing out over the kirkyard – the largest carillon in Britain.

The list of top people buried in the old kirkyard goes on and on . . . John Anderson, the Wizard of the North (see Chapter 20); William Dyce, the painter; Andrew Cant, the Covenanting minister known as 'Bobbin Andrew' because he jerked about in his pulpit; the Rev. James Kidd, a well-known cleric who, irritated by a man who repeatedly coughed during his sermon, declared that some folk came to kirk once a week just to clear their throats; the ship-owning family of Roses, whose Hazlehead estate is now one of the most popular parks in the city; and many more.

But there are other stones with sad little tales attached to them. Up in a quiet corner of the cemetery near the Correction Wynd wall is a stone to Alexander Skene and his family. Skene was the Superintendent of the Jhansi presidency of Bengal, who died at the age of forty, and the stone tells the story of how his young wife, Beatrice, and her two infant daughters were murdered during the Indian Mutiny.

At the back of the church is a stone to the Drowned Soldiers. These were four young soldiers of the Royal Highlanders who were drowned while bathing off Aberdeen Beach in May 1864. The stone was erected by the Army friends and their names were Acting Corporal John McCracken and Privates James McBridie, Donald and William Forbes. When they lived, they could never had imagined that one day they would be buried in St Nicholas churchyard alongside the Great and the Good from the Granite City.

18
PRINCE'S MUSICAL CHAIRS

Down in a triangle of grass at Union Terrace, Aberdeen, the Prince Consort sits in a heavy Gothic chair that seems too large for him, his legs encased in long jack-boots that seem too big for him. He wears the uniform of a field-marshal, with the robe and insignia of the Order of the Thistle, but he has a pensive, faraway look, almost as if he was pondering on why his statue is there at all.

The truth is that it wasn't always there. Prince Albert got caught up in a game of musical chairs played by the civic authorities, who shifted royal statues about (and a few commoners with them) as if they thought it unwise to leave them hanging about on the same spot too long.

Prince Albert originally stood, or sat, at the junction of Union Terrace and Union Street. Baron Marochetti, the sculptor, was allowed to chose the site of the statue and plumped for Union Terrace. On a wet, miserable morning on Tuesday October 13, 1863, Queen Victoria and members of the Royal Family travelled from Balmoral to attend the unveiling of the statue, which sat on a massive granite pedestal.

An elegy had been written for the occasion, dripping with cloying, over-ripe verse in a last tribute to 'that Good Prince whom all men loved so well' and paying loyal tribute to the Queen 'in the chambers of her silent woes':

> Men pay not gifts of love! Both heart and hand
> Have done their work, to future times to tell
> Of that calm front familiar to the land –
> Of that Good Prince whom all men loved so well.

> But we who saw him in his rich ripe years –
> As greatly good, as he was goodly great –
> Look inward, where his form to memory wears
> The grace of manhood, royal as his state.

> Although his sun was darkened at its noon,
> The golden wheat, upon his Summer fields,
> In full ear'd swathes. All harvested so soon,
> Bore fruits as rich as ever autumn yields.

Statue of Prince Albert at Union Terrace.

The day had been declared a general holiday and huge crowds gathered in the streets, which were lined by the military and volunteers. The Queen, dressed in deep mourning, travelled from Balmoral to Aboyne by coach, where a special train was waiting to take her to Guild Street station in Aberdeen. There, she boarded a carriage drawn by four horses and was taken to her husband's statue.

In Union Street, directly opposite the Terrace, a grandstand capable of seating 500 people had been erected. It was filled by 'a fashionable assemblage of ladies and gentlemen'. The Royal Northern Club at the corner of Union Terrace had been set aside for the use of the Royal Family. Lord Provost Alexander Anderson presented the Queen with an address from the contributors to the memorial, then knelt before her and had a knighthood conferred on him.

Aberdeen presented a dreich face to the royal visitors that day, adding to the gloom of the occasion. The rain poured down on their arrival, splattered down on the wet platform during the unveiling, and sent them home again with another downpour. Victoria wrote in her *Journal* about 'the long, sad and terrible procession through the crowded streets of Aberdeen, where all were kindly, but all were silent and mournful'. Unfortunately, she said, it continued pouring.

It was obvious from her notes that Victoria wasn't completely happy with Marochetti's work. 'The place where the Statue is placed is rather small,' she wrote, 'and on one side close to the bridge, but Marochetti chose it himself.' It stood, in fact, only a few feet from the kerb, roughly where there are now traffic lights.

She also thought that the statue was 'rather small for out-of-doors'.

The queen wasn't the only one with reservations about the statue. Although Marochetti was at the peak of his fame in 1863, his work on the bronze sculpture of the Prince Consort was not well received. It was said that the Gothic chair of state was 'unduly prominent', as were the jackboots he wore. Sir William Geddes, Principal of Aberdeen University, said that the statue was 'not a man in a chair, but a chair with a man in it'.

The Aberdeen historian William Robbie, writing in 1891, said that opinion was from the first divided on the merits of the statue as a work of art. 'It is sometimes the case that such a work comes to be more thought of as we get to know it better, but in this instance we rather think that the tendency has been in the opposite direction.'

'It has been sarcastically remarked,' he went on, 'that the most prominent feature of the figure is a pair of huge jack boots, and though this is only an exaggerated way of speaking, it is generally held that the work as a whole is not much of a success.

'We believe, however, that the unfavourable impression produced by this statue is due mainly to the figure being placed in a sitting position, which particularly in the open air is not good for effect. In the present case the body seems quite buried in a big chair, so that there is little to be seen but the legs and the head, and the latter, owing to the breadth imparted to the body by profuse drapery, looks too small and out of proportion to the other parts.

'But the facial likeness is good and had the erect position been chosen for the sculptor's work, or had the pedestal been lower so as to bring the face and figure more in line with the eye of the spectator, it would have been far more effective.'

They were still at it half a century after the statue had been unveiled. It was said 'time has not modified the feeling of disappointment.'

William Wallace, also at Union Terrace.

So poor Albert was ignominiously kicked out of his seat, shunted off to the other end of Union Terrace to make way for his son, King Edward VII. He is still there today, unnoticed and dwarfed by William Wallace, less than a stone's throw away.

Oddly enough, the City Fathers also played musical chairs with Wallace's statue, which was designed by W. Grant Stevenson in 1888. The original intention was to put the statue on the Mound in the Duthie Park, a site chosen with the guidance of Her Majety's Limner, Sir Noel Paton, and the architect Rowand Anderson.

The Town Council sent a deputation to visit a full-size plaster model of the statue in Stevenson's studio. The deputation was so impressed with it that they decided that a more prominent location should be found for it. They picked a little precinct at the end of Rosemount Viaduct. The monument was opened by the Marquis of Lorne on 29 June, 1888 and the Marquis was given the freedom of the city.

The choice of the site for Wallace's statue was a good one – good, that is, until Education, Salvation and Damnation descended on this corner of the city. This was the name given to three buildings erected there in the early 1890s. Education was the Central Library, built in 1891, and Salvation rose next to it a year later. Damnation, of course, was His Majestys's Theatre.

Across the street, William Wallace now stood with his arm outstretched as if pointing the way to the back stalls and the Gods. Not long ago, when conservation work was carried out on the statue it was discovered that the cast-iron core of the figure was completely eroded and the statue itself was now hollow. Scotland's hero, it seemed, could stomach no more.

It was ironic that when Prince Albert was moved to his present stance, his father, Edward VII, landed up at the Union Terrace–Union Street junction because he himself had been considered for another site – and had been rejected. His statue was originally intended as the centrepiece of the Cowdray Hall quadrant, but the Victorian obsession with monarchical sculptures had faded away after the First World War. The proposal to put Edward at the Cowdray Hall had little public support, so off he went to displace his father from the prime site in Union Terrace.

The move to Union Terrace did Edward little good. The architect Arthur Clyne, who was responsible for many notable granite buildings in the late 19th and early 20th century, was strongly opposed to the use of granite for the King's monument, and Lewis Grassic Gibbon thought that Edward's statue was 'merely vulgar'. The Aberdeen poet Alistair Mackie dismissed him as 'that fat clort'.

Aberdonians have always argued endlessly about the placing and composition of their statues. Queen Victoria herself has been caught up in these 'musical chairs' over the years. In 1866 a Sicilian marble statue of the Queen was erected at the south-east corner of St Nicholas Street and Union Street. It was this statue, unveiled by her son Edward, when Prince of Wales, that gave birth to a greeting that was to echo down through generations, 'See you at the Queen!' In 1888 the Queen was moved into a vestibule in the Town House because twenty years of Aberdeen weather had begun to damage her marble limbs.

In 1893 there was a new Queen Victoria on the St Nicholas site, made of bronze. It stayed there until 1964, when it was sent off to Queen's Cross, where Victoria could gaze westwards towards her beloved Balmoral. When there was talk of a new Park and Ride route coming down Queen's Road, there were rumours that her Majesty might be on the move again, but it never happened.

The year before Victoria was plumped down on the St Nicholas site, a new statue took her place in the Union Terrace gallery. Rabbie Burns, who once said that Aberdeen was 'a lazy town', was stuck up on a pedestal holding a daisy. Some nameless vandals kept pinching his daisy, but the City Fathers always dutifully replaced it. They must have found a way of making it theft-proof, for no one has had a go at it for some time.

Meanwhile, farther down the Terrace the 'chair with a man in it' remains in place. When I am passing, I sometimes look up and wonder what thoughts might be going through his bronze head. He is probably thinking that when he was alive people thought he was too big for his boots, but when he died all they could say was that his boots were too big for him!

19
THE OLD BAND BOX

Two centuries have passed since an army of bootless feet stamped out a demand for 'Music! Music!' as the curtain rose in the Old Band Box in Marischal Street. They played to packed houses then, but those good old days have long since gone. Today, the only indication that the Band Box ever existed is a sign in a narrow close between Regent Quay and Virginia Streeet. It says 'Theatre Lane'.

The Old Band-Box was the name given to the Theatre Royal, the city's first permanent theatre, and its rear entrance was in Theatre Lane. This old house was looked upon as the early home of drama in Scotland – the ground on which many famous actors and actresses began their careers. It was said to be 'a somewhat curious fact' that in the days of the stage-coach more performers came north to Aberdeen, with its population of 25,000, than there were in the days of the railway nearly eighty years later, when the population had risen to 88,120.

There were theatres, or playhouses, in Aberdeen long before the Band Box opened in 1795. In 1768 a hall was fitted up as a theatre in the New Inn, and in 1780 another theatre was built at the back of an inn in Queen Street. One of the curious features of the Queen Street theatre was a chair placed in the centre of the second row of benches in the gallery. Here, an eccentric schoolmaster known as Mad Sinclair led the applause – or called on patrons to show their disapproval.

Coachy's Playhouse was run by a coach proprietor called Sutherland in Chronicle Lane, and down in Exchange Street there was the Alhambra. The Music Hall offered opposition to the Old Band Box; not the Music Hall of today, but Macfarlane's Music Hall in Market Street. There was also a small theatre in Shoe Lane.

But the Aberdeen Theatre, known as the Old Band-Box and later as the Theatre Royal, was the best of them all. It cost £3000 to build in 1795 and could seat 600 people. Not everybody liked it; its stage was small and so was its auditorium – and the acting of the stock companies who played there in the early days left a lot to be desired. Edwin Waugh, a Lancashire poet who went to the Theatre

Theatre Lane – a link with the Old Band Box, the Theatre Royal.

Royal to see a performance of *Ingomar the Barbarian*, or *The Son of the Wilderness*, said that the woodwork looked as if it had been made out of old orange boxes and ruined market stalls.

'The check-taker looked like a worn-out bum-bailiff,' he wrote. 'The tragedy was a farce, the comedy was downright murder, and the music sounded like an accompaniment to tooth-drawing.' There were 'three split fiddles and a hoarse cornopean [a musical horn]' in the orchestra and the last tune they played was reminiscent of a dog-battle. The actor playing the barbarian was seen 'taking a strong pull at something in a pitcher' when Waugh left.

Yet, unbelievably, Waugh enjoyed it. 'It was so gloriously ill-done that it was impossible not to be pleased with it,' he said. 'The play's the thing', said Shakespeare, but there was a lot more to it than that at the Old Band Box. In 18th-century Aberdeen theatre-going was a joyous occasion in which eating and drinking was as much part of the fun as over-the-top performances and curtain calls. There was plenty of audience participation, but it usually took the form of shouting abuse at the actors or pelting the orchestra with mutton pies.

There was a shop at the top of Marischal Street called 'Hoastie' Bain's, where people bought pastries and sweets on their way to the theatre. The county gentry's carriages often drew up at the shop, where 'Hoastie' would be waiting for them dressed in a black coat, a lum hat and a long white apron reaching to his feet. He got his nickname because his conversation was always punctuated by short coughs. Nobody knew if they were caused by bad health or a bad habit.

If you didn't get your refreshments at 'Hoastie's' you got them from 'Candy John' inside the theatre. This was John M'Lean, an amateur actor who took part in some of the plays. He ran a candy stall in the New Market, but also had a refreshment room in the Old Band Box pit. The boys in the gallery gave him a hard time. When he spoke the line, 'Where shall I hide him?' in one of the plays, a voice from the Gods rang out, 'Put him under the candy stall, John!' Another of Candy's lines, 'Give me a dagger!' brought a shout from the gallery, 'Give him a stalk of candy!'

'Up wi' the hippin'!' shouted the lads in the gallery on opening night. 'Hippins' were nappies – and 'hippins' were what they called the stage curtain. They stamped their feet, demanded music, complained about the delay, and yelled for 'Maggie Shinnie's Rant', a song about an old woman who kept a sweetmeat stall in Castle Street. Among them was Mrs D–, the Queen of the Gallery. She was a schoolmaster's widow who had a season ticket for the gallery and always occupied the front seat. When she arrived the message went out – 'Mak' way there, mak' way for the Queen!'

'They had no scented programmes in this rudely-manner house,' wrote J. Keith Angus in a pamphlet about the old Theatre Royal. Instead, they had long play-bills, finger-coloured from the printer's ink. 'It was, as a diversion between acts, a common practice to tear these into strips and, fastening them end to end, to dangle the paper string from the gallery to the pit, where their reception met with extreme merriment; or to tickle the heads and faces of the front row in the dress circle, where their reception caused infinite disgust and annoyance.

Aberdeen theatre audiences had, and still have, a reputation for being ultra-critical of visiting companies. If productions pass the test in the Granite City, they will do well anywhere. This attitude must have drifted down from the days of the Old Band Box. 'They knew when to cheer,' wrote J. Keith Angus, 'but they were uncharitable enough to know when to sneer and deride, these hard-heated critics in the classical city of the north.'

William Carnie, in his *Reporting Reminiscences,* described the Theatre Royal as it was in 1850. There were three admission doors. When you stepped through the main centre door you were in the 'box circle', looking straight forward to the stage, which receded to Theatre Lane. The circle ran round from wing to wing of the stage and looked into the pit, where you could have a chat with anyone seated there.

The pay-box was manned by 'a good old mason's labourer', who delivered play-bills during the day and took the gallery cash at night. A steep, cranky stair took patrons to the left-hand side of the gallery, but to get to the right-hand side they had to go through a low-roofed dark passage – 'a tunnel in fact', said Cairnie – where there was a gaslight which was usually turned off by the first people into the gallery. Higher up were a couple of seated enclosures nearly touching the roof which were called the 'Sweeps' Boxes'.

The performances at began at seven o'clock in the evening and lasted until five minutes before midnight. Sometimes, they went on to one o'clock in the morning. 'We would have demanded our money back had we been dismissed earlier,' wrote William Skene in his *East Neuk Chronicles.* 'We would have had to be ejected by the policeman, or rather the man with the policeman's coat on, and then there would have been war, as we did not give much heed to the officer. He was employed principally for the purpose of stopping smoking, but the boys used to light their pipes and laugh at him.'

It was Corbet Ryder, a Welshman, who raised the old theatre to greater heights. He took over as manager in 1827 and ran it successfully until his death in 1842. His widow married John Pollock, a member of the stock company, who died in 1853. After that, Mrs Ryder held it until 1862. The Ryders and their family were said to be 'as well-known in their day as the town house clock'.

Ryder brought every prominent actor of the day to the city at one time or another. In 1828, when he persuaded Edmund Kean to come to Aberdeen to play Richard III, the prices were doubled. William

A
SELECTION
OF
FAVOURITE SONGS,
AS SUNG AT THE
Theatre-Royal, Aberdeen,
BY

MISS NOEL,	MR SINCLAIR,
MISS DYER,	MR WEEKES,
MISS HOLMES,	MR FELTON,

&c.

WITH A PORTRAIT OF MR SINCLAIR,

As Orlando in "The Cabinet."

ABERDEEN :
LEWIS SMITH, 78, BROAD STREET.
1827.

Mr SINCLAIR AS ORLANDO.

A programme from the Theatre Royal.

Charles Macready; John Philip Kemble, the tragedian; Daniel Terry, the comedian; and Sheridan Knowles, the playright, were among the celebrities who came north to the theatre.

Corbet Ryder's son, Tom, a talented actor who threw away many opportunies of reaching the top of his profession, was a favourite with Theatre Royal audiences. He died at the age of sixty-one in 1872 – 'his last part is played', said his obituary notice, 'the curtain has fallen on him for ever'.

The Theatre Royal had also come to the end of its time. 'The curtain of the well remembered old home of drama in Marischal Street', wrote William Carnie, 'was rung down for the last time, season 1872–73'. It was replaced by Her Majesty's Opera House in Guild Street (later called Her Majesty's Theatre) and eventually by His Majesty's Theatre, under the managership of H. Adair Nelson.

But memories of the good old days of the Theatre Royal, and of how it had carved out a distinguished place for itself in the world of drama, lingered on. In 1876, a benefit was arranged for Emma Ryder, Corbet Ryder's daughter and wife of Edward Price, one of the company's actors. In it, Emma urged her listeners to 'maintain the Drama's honoured cause' –

> See that it moves in dignity's clear sheen,
> Worthy of you and classic Aberdeen.
> Think of your grand traditions – history's page
> Records that Keans and Kembles trod your stage:
> Sheridan Knowles his own plays did reveal,
> And boastful plaudits greeted great O'Neil.

Today, the theatre is the home of the Elim Pentecostal Church and Theatre Lane is the entrance to an emergency centre for the homeless. Inside this gloomy little alley there are no links with the days of the Old Band Box, but if you listen hard enough, and your imagination is strong enough, you may hear the sound of thumping feet, the scraping of fiddles and the sonorous tones of a coropean, and a cry drifting down the years – 'Up wi' the hippin'!'

20
ABERDEEN'S TWO DEVILS

With his waxed moustache curving up from his lip like a pair of horns, his grey lum hat tilted at a rakish angle on his coal-black hair, his cloak billowing behind him like a black cloud, Dr Walford Bodie, M.D., the great illusionist, must have looked as if he was in league with the Devil – or, even worse, that he was Aul' Nick himself. He never denied it. When people challenged him about the letters after his name he always claimed that they stood for Merry Devil.

Three years after Bodie was born, John H. Anderson died. An illusionist like Bodie, he had dominated the entertainment world in Aberdeen for over half a century. He called himself 'Professor', which may have given Bodie the idea of adopting the title 'Doctor'. Anderson was also regarded by nervous old ladies as Satan. One landlady, on learning who he was, said she could smell the brimstone on him. She handed him back the four half-crowns he had paid in advance and told him to go. 'The De'il's in my pouch dancing wi' the half-croons,' she declared.

Both men called themselves wizards. John Anderson became known as the Wizard of the North, while Walford Bodie billed himself as The Great Electric Wizard. Between them they mesmerised, confused, amused, puzzled and sometimes angered audiences all over the country – and abroad – for more than a century.

John Henry Anderson, whose parents were cottars at Kincardine O'Neil on Deeside, picked up conjuring from 'Old Scottie', an odd character who ran Scotties's Show in Aberdeen's John Street, where you could enjoy an evening's entertainment for a penny. William Carnie, in his *Reporting Reminiscences*, said that as a sleight-of-hand artist Anderson lacked the skill and originality of his contemporaries, yet his reputation 'surpassed them all by miles'. The reason – he was a high-class master in the art of advertising.

He showed his talent for self-publicity while on a visit to Deeside. At the Brig o' Potarch he came upon a number of men cutting peat. He started chatting to them and during their conversation he remarked that silver and gold could be found in peat mosses. 'I saw silver on that peat there,' he said. 'Hand it to me and I'll break it.'

Walford Bodie.

He took the peat, broke it, and out rolled a silver sixpence. 'Hand me that one,' he told another peat-cutter. Again, the peat was broken and out fell a shilling. Finally, he took a spade and cut a peat himself. This time a sovereign fell out. Anderson left the money with the labourers. They had no idea that he had fooled them with sleight-of-hand, but when it was learned that the Wizard had been at Banchory the story of his 'magic' at the peat moss soon got around. It was said that it did him more good on Deeside than any paid-for advertising.

Anderson once amazed Queen Victoria at Balmoral by producing out of the air hats, bird cages, a live goose, goldfish in bowls, and his own son Oscar in full Highland dress. The young Prince of Wales was said to have described with glee how the Wizard of the North had 'cut to pieces mama's pocket-handkerchief'.

The prince went on to tell how Anderson had darned the handkerchief and ironed it 'so that it was as entire as ever'. He also spoke about the Wizard firing a pistol and 'causing five or six watches go through Gibb's head'. Gibb was a footman, but Albert Edward wasn't entirely convinced, for he remarked that if the watches had really gone through his head he could hardly have

ERECTED
BY
JOHN ANDERSON,
IN MEMORY OF
HIS BELOVED MOTHER,
MARY ROBERTSON,
WHO DIED 8TH JANUARY,
1830, AGED 40.
Yes! She had friends when
fortune smil'd: it frown'd
they knew her not! She died
the Orphans weept but liv'd to
mark this Hallow'd Spot.
HERE ALSO RESTS THE ABOVE
JOHN ANDERSON
WIZARD OF THE NORTH,
DIED 3RD, FEBRUARY 1874
AGED 60.

John Anderson's tombstone.

looked so well. 'Papa', said the prince knowingly, 'knows how all these things are done.'

Anderson's masterpiece was 'the great gun trick', which he was taught by Scottie, whose daughter he eventually married. He performed it as an interlude between the dramas in the show. He himself often dressed in the kilt to play the part of Rob Roy, for despite his success as an illusionist he had a secret ambition to become a great actor. It was said that he performed all over the world. He was in the Antipodes when gold was first discovered there, and his bills were posted on the Pyramids in Egypt.

William Carnie, who knew him well, said his life was a wayward one. 'He was a strange mortal, a remarkable mixture,' he wrote. He performed before all the crowned heads of Europe, but he knew poverty. When he died in Darlington in 1874 at the age of sixty, there was nothing left to give away apart from a few pieces of conjuring equipment. But some people must have thought otherwise – three women turned up each claiming to be his widow.

Walford Bodie wasn't all *he* was made out to be either. His real name was Sam Murphy, but he changed it for his stage career and took the name Walford from a Werner Walford who married his sister. His medical degrees, which included a Ph.D. amd D.Sc., were from the Barrett College, New York, and were highly suspect. A group of medical students in Glasgow took exception to them when he appeared at the Coliseum. There were ugly scenes and a number of students were arrested.

His first professional appearance was at Stonehaven Town Hall in 1884. Like the Wizard of the North, his main skill was sleight-of-hand, but a newspaper report in 1889 also listed cartooning and ventriloquism among his talents. Later, he introduced hypnotism into his act, putting a man into a trance for a week – 'watched day and night by a committee,' he reassured his public.

When he left school he became apprenticed to the National Telephone Company, which gave him an insight into electricity. He put this to electrifying use when he introduced his Cage of Death to an awe-struck audience in Glasgow. He billed it as

BODIE'S CAGE OF DEATH

Featuring the Dreaded Death Chair
Bodie's passing of 30,000 volts of
eletricity through his body.

The Cage of Death was an electric chair brought over from Sing Sing after an American tour. Although Bodie passed 30,000 volts through his body, the current was said to be negligible. During the performance a coffin was taken on stage and placed near the orchestra railing.

He was billed as the Great Electric Wizard. He used electro-therapy and hypnosis to cure the sick, taking no fee but asking his patients to leave their crutches or aids with him. They were put on show inside and outside the theatres in which he worked. He claimed that after curing a deformed youth, 200 cripples came to see him the following day.

Bodie was assisted in his acts by 'the accomplished Jeannie Henri'. This in fact, was a Macduff girl, Jeannie Henry, who married Bodie when she was only eighteen. Writing in 1929 about her life with the

Electric Wizard, she said: 'I predict that hypnotism will play an important part in medical science'. Seventy years later, her prophecy is coming true.

Mrs Bodie's brother-in-law, Tom Norman Mills, himself a music hall entertainer, became the 'Doctor's' manager. Bodie's sister was the 'Mystic Marie' of one of his acts and one of his wife's relatives, whom he called La Belle Electra, took part in his hypnotism acts. On one occasion she was hypnotised, put in a coffin, and buried 6 feet under the ground. She was left in her 'grave' for 20 minutes, and when the earth was removed and the coffin hauled out she stepped out none the worse for her experience.

Bodie adopted Macduff as his home, building an extravagant 'pebble house' which is still there today. His daughter, Jeannie, died and Bodie erected a memorial fountain to her, placed near the harbour at first and later moved to Duff Street. But there is no memorial to the Great Electric Wizard. He is virtually forgotten in his adopted town.

Aberdeen's two Devils made fortunes and lost them. For them, Life was the Great Illusion – they ended their days in poverty and obscurity. As tastes in entertainment changed, Walford Bodie, now into his sixties, ran into money troubles and was faced with mounting debts and ill health.

In January, 1937, he took to the stage for a 'final appearance' at the Tivoli in Guild Street. In the *Press & Journal* of Tuesday 26 January, an advertisement announced the 'Farewell Engagement of one of the World's Greatest Variety Personalities':

THE ONE AND ONLY

Dr Walford Bodie
assisted by his
Original Medium
'Electra'

There were a number of supporting acts, including that of Charlton's Marionettes and the Bashful Boys.

Bodie never returned to Aberdeen. In the autumn of 1939 he collapsed while appearing at the old Indian Theatre in Blackpool. He was rushed to hospital but it was too late. The man who had billed himself as the Miracle Worker was beyond miracles. He died on 19 October 1939. His body was embalmed and taken north to Macduff for burial.

John Anderson was buried in St Nicholas Churchyard beside his mother, who died at the age of forty. Forty-four years earlier, he had inscribed a curious verse on her tombstone:

> Yes, she had friends when fortune smiled;
> It frowned, they knew her not;
> She died, the orphans wept
> But lived to mark this hallowed spot.

No one knows what lay behind those bitter lines. William Carnie said that Alexander had requested in his last hours 'to be laid in the half-hidden lair in our St Nicholas Churchyard, where in years long gone by he had reverently buried his mother'. But he made no mention of the inscription on the headstone.

Carnie helped to bury Anderson. 'The coffin was the only one of its make I ever saw,' he wrote, 'the lid having an open glass-covered square through which the face of the corpse could be distinctly seen.' The Wizard of the North had made his exit in style.

21
THEREBY HANGS A TAIL

How long is an elephant's tail?

That question has its roots in one of the strangest stories ever to come out of the Gordon Highlanders Museum in Aberdeen. The setting for the tale – or tail – is Ceylon, now Sri Lanka, and the hero is a soldier who gloried in the name of Captain (later Sir) Ernest Beckwith Beachcroft Towse. Most people called him 'Beach'.

Early in his career, when Captain Towse was stationed in India, he took part in what was a popular pastime for army officers – elephant hunting. On one occasion he went hunting in Ceylon and, having bagged his elephant, cut off its tail as a trophy. Making his way back to camp on his own he got lost. For two nights he was without food as he tried to find his way back.

How did he survive? The answer can be found in an exhibit in the Gordon Highlanders museum – the elephant's tail. 'Beach' kept up his strength as he struggled through the jungle by eating his trophy, or, at least, part of it.

The tail, which is on display in a glass case in the museum, is about 2 inches thick, with hard bristles or hair at its tip. It measures 52 cm (1-foot 8-inches), but there is nothing to indicate its original length, or to show how much of it Captain Towse ate. To get some idea you have to find the average length of a Jumbo's tail. That presents problems, for the experts say it depends on whether it is an Indian elephant or an African elephant, the only two species of elephant still surviving.

Illustrations of both African and Asian elephants show that Indian elephants have shorter tails. In other words, if 'Beach' had shot his Jumbo in Africa he would have had more tail meat to carry him through his ordeal. But it was an Indian elephant that fell to his gun.

The Natural History Department of the Royal Scottish Museum in Edinburgh said that the length of a male Asian elephant's tail was from 1.5 m (approx 3 feet) to 2.1 m (approx 6-feet). They have a female Asian elephant in the museum with a tail measuring 1.3 m (4 feet), but that is considered unusually short.

Captain Beechcroft Towse.

So, based on the longest average length, 6 feet, Captain Towse ate 2 feet of his Jumbo's tail – two thirds of it. It could never have appeased his hunger, for the Royal Scottish Museum spokesman said there would have been very little eating in it. But it was enough to save the life of a man who was to become one of the greatest Gordon Highlanders.

Ernest Beckwith Beachcroft Towse's tale didn't end in the jungles of Ceylon. He fought in the South African War and was awarded the Victoria Cross for gallantry on two separate occasions. The first was at Magersfontein, when he attempted to rescue a wounded comrade at great risk to his own life.

The second was at Mount Thaba, when he found himself facing 150 of the enemy with only thirteen men at his side. Ignoring a call to surrender, Towse rushed his men forward, firing all the way.

Left: The elephant's tail. Right: Stuart Allan, curator, with the elephant's tail.

Incredibly, the enemy turned and fled. But Towse paid a cruel price for his bravery. He was shot in the face and blinded.

Later, the incident was recalled by General Smith Dorrien. 'I shall never forget the pathetic sight of the stricken Towse,' he said, 'shot through both eyes; certain he would never see again, not a thought for himself, but plenty for his men, hoping that he had done his duty, and with it all so cheerful and apparently happy.'

Captain Towse received the Victoria Cross from Queen Victoria herself. It is said that when he went to Windsor to receive the award, the Queen was so overcome with emotion that she burst into tears.

This remarkable Gordon Highlander, blind though he was, served in yet another battlefield. Determined to overcome his disability, he devoted his life to the welfare of the blind. During the First World War he went to the front in France to help soldiers who had been blinded like himself. He worked without pay at field and base hospitals, visiting the wounded, typing letters for them from his braille notes, and giving them hope through his own positive attitude.

Captain Towse is one of many Gordon Highlanders whose bravery is mirrored in the pictures and stories to be seen in the museum. Among these heroes of the past is Pipe-Major Alexander Cameron, who was driven by *mire chath*, the frenzy of battle, when an enemy bullet struck his beloved bagpipes at the Pass of Maya during the Spanish Peninsular War in 1813.

When the bullet pierced the bag of his pipes it gave out 'a piteous and unwarlike skirl'. It was worse than a human cry to the pipe-major – and it was an insult to his music. He tied his pipes round his neck and declared, 'Bheir sinn ceol dannsaidh eile dhaibh (We will give them a different kind of dance music).' Then he drew his sword and rushed into the thick of the fighting cheered on by his comrades.

There was no VC for Pipe-Major Cameron, but his outstanding courage and humour in the face of danger was recognised by the award of a special medal. The inscription on it read: 'Presented to Pipe Major Alexander Cameron by the officers of the Regiment. A reward for his gallant conduct in the Peninsula.'

22
GOODLY AND GODLY

Aberdeen's newest hostelry and restaurant is housed in the former Clydesdale Bank (originally the North Bank of Scotland) at the corner of Union Street and King Street. It has been named after the man who designed the old North Bank – Archibald Simpson, the city's greatest architect. When Simpson drew up plans for the bank, a well-known city tavern had to be demolished to make way for it. It was called the New Inn.

There is, however, a curious twist to the story. If things had gone ahead as originally planned, the North Bank would never have been built. Instead, another hotel would have been standing on the Castle Street site. This was because the owners of the New Inn had planned to demolish it and erect a large new inn more in keeping with the times. Simpson was engaged to design it and a plan showing the accommodation on the ground floor was actually drawn up.

The plan was never used. In 1839, the North of Scotland Bank stepped in and acquired the ground for its new head office. The building of a modernised New Inn was scrapped – and Archibald Simpson got down to the business of planning a bank instead of a pub.

Aberdeen ended up with a building that was said to be the finest in the city – Simpson himself regarded it as his masterpiece – but the community was robbed of a hostelry that had served it for over eighty years. It was built in 1755 by the Aberdeen Lodge of Freemasons, who took the upper storey as a hall for their meetings. To avoid clashing with the inn's customers at the front entrance they made another entrance at the back. This meant laying out a lane linking up with the adjoining streets. Its name – Lodge Walk.

The New Inn played host to some famous people. Boswell and Johnson stopped there on their trip to the Western Isles in 1773 – and found that it was full up. 'Boswell made himself known', wrote Dr Johnson, 'and *his* name over-powered all objections. We found a very good house and civil treatment'. In 1787, Robert Burns 'drank a glass' there with Bishop Skinner and James Chalmers, editor of the *Aberdeen Journal*, and 'discussed the national poetry over the national liquor'. George Coleman, the famous dramatist, stared out of the New Inn's windows at a Highland Regiment of Fencibles 'dolefully drawn up in the drizzling rain, ankle-deep in mud'. The drone of bagpipes, said Coleman, 'kept *Maggy Lauder*-ing and *Lochaber no more*-ing, enough to drive its hearers melancholy mad'.

In those days, there were no cars and buses rumbling down Castle Street; only the occasional horse, with a lum-hatted rider on its back, disturbed the pedestrian peace. The town's Top People walked and talked and took their ease on the Plainstones, doffing their top hats to the ladies. In 1806, a drawing master called Robert Seaton, a man with a keen eye for business, decided to cash in on this Plainstones Parade. He held a lottery in which the prize was 'A view of the Castle Street of Aberdeen on a Market Day'. Ticket No. 67 was drawn and an unknown lady carried off the picture. It was later sold to the Town Council and hung in the Town House and today it is in the keeping of the city's Art Gallery.

Seaton's picture shows the name in front of the New Inn – 'New Inn, Tavern and Hotel. E. Cleugh'. One major feature of the picture was that its crowd scene contained 'some well-known characters in Aberdeen'. A tall 'personage' chatting to two ladies was said to be John Ewen, a local jeweller, and near him is the Rev. Alexander Alcock, of St Paul's Episcopal Chapel. But not all the 'characters' were top people, for in one corner of the picture Watty Leith, the town drummer, is seen banging away at his drum, while across the street John Milne, the town's hangman, is claiming from a fishwife the fish that was part of his 'perks'.

In 1840, a local businessman, John Hay, went one better. He published a picture of Castle Street which showed the North of Scotland Bank 'as it will appear when Mr Simpson's elegantly designed building shall have been completed'. Taking a leaf from Smeaton's book, he filled the Castlegate with 'striking portraits of our best-known and most respectable citizens'.

Everybody who was anybody appeared in Hay's print. Provost James Hadden, who was then said to be 'old and venerable', is seen being approached by two Town House officials, and James Johnston, manager of the Aberdeen Bank (now the Bank of Scotland) at the corner of Marischal Street, has come out to have a look at his new rival, the North Bank. The artist probably had in mind a poem about Johnston written by John Ramsay, editor of the *Aberdeen Journal*:

Forth from his mansion – just at ten o'clock –
Struts the learned Banker, like a turkey cock.

The Provost of the time, James Milne, is seen making his way to the Athenaeum with the town officer, Simon Grant, and Dr Joseph Robertson, the noted historian, is there with James Adam, the editor of the *Aberdeen Herald,* and Ignatius Massie, an auctioneer who became manager of the Gasworks. Two knights can be seen – Sir Alexander Bannerman and Sir Michael Bruce of Scotston, the latter on horseback. John Angus, the town clerk, is making his way to the Town House and nearby is John Hay, the publisher of the print. One man is seen going up the steps into the North Bank – Henry Paterson, a 'bold and daring speculator'. There were wild rumours that Paterson was so rich that he manured his fields with bank notes.

The portraits of the 'best-known and respectable citizens' in Hay's print were done by 'Mr P. Mackenzie, a young and talented artist'. Perhaps another young and talented artist of the new millennium will come forward to do the same for the Archibald Simpson restaurant. Lord Provost Farquhar could be seen chatting to the ratepayers about the Common Good Fund, our old friend Alex Collie, one-time Links and Parks convener and former Lord Provost, could sport a rose in his buttonhole as a reminder of the city's Britain in Bloom successes, and burly Bob Middleton, who is known as something of a poet, could do a John Ramsay and be seen writing a poem about Ceres, the Goddess of Plenty, who sits on her pedestal above the entrance to the building, looking like Britannia on the back of an old penny.

With Ceres keeping an eye on everything, the Archibald Simpson, which will serve food all day, will have to look to its laurels. Eating and drinking was a serious business in the old days – particularly drinking. In 1889, a discussion was carried out in the local papers about how much liquor was consumed by thirty-one people, councillors and others, at an inspection of the Aberdeen Waterworks.

This made an anonymous reader, A.W., look up some old tavern bills, one of which showed the amount of 'good honest liquor' consumed by forty-two people at a dinner in the New Inn in November, 1795. A.W. had a list of the people present. 'It is a goodly and a godly roll,' he wrote. 'There is a Provost, three Baillies, a Bishop, four Parish Ministers and Professors, two Collectors of

Taxes, Landed Proprietors, Merchants, Manufacturers and others.'
The host was William Gordon, and this was the bill:

NEW INN, ABERDEEN.
Mr. _____

1795.

5th Nov.	Entertainment	£5	0	0
	22 Bo. Port	3	6	0
	12,, Sherry	2	2	0
	80,, Claret	18	0	0
	Porter and Beer	0	11	0
	Brandy	0	3	0
	Almonds and Raisins	0	11	6
	Broken Glass	0	0	2
		£29	15	6
30th Nov.	Bottle Claret	0	4	6
		£30	0	0
	Servants	1	0	0
		£31	0	0

New Inn, Aberdeen,
　30th November, 1795.
　　　　Settled the above,
　　　　W. Gordon.

Were our City Fathers suffering from terrible hangovers the next
day? Not at all! 'These fathers of the city', wrote A.W., 'the morning
after the 5th of November dinner, were calm, cool, collected. No
customary shutter was needed at night, no absence from the desk on
the morrow.'

There was no shortage of eating and drinking places in this corner
of the city. Some years before the New Inn was demolished in 1840,
the building of King Street had swept away the Flesh Market, the
Poultry Market and the Meal Market, and with them the curiously-
named Luxembourg Close, a thoroughfare linking these markets
with Castle Street. The Close was known for its celebrated tap-room,
the 'howff' of William Beattie, the poet – 'and other wags and wits
of the time'.

If the New Inn was the most popular inn, the Lemon Tree Hotel
in nearby Huxter Row was close on its heels. George Walker, a
well-known bookseller and author of *Aberdeen Awa'*, thought that
if Rabbie Burns or Dr Johnson had stayed there they would have left
the city with more favourable impressions than they did. The clergy

The new Archibald Simpson restaurant, formerly the Clydesdale Bank (North Bank), at the corner of King Street and Union Street. It carries on a tradition set by the New Inn last century.

plumped for the Lemon Tree, and the reason for this was made clear in a poem written in 1813 about a Synod meeting in Aberdeen. It told what happened after the brothers had 'digested their wrongs':

> And now methinks at four I see
> The brethren all in 'Lemon Tree',
> For here, they fail not to convene,
> Round Ronald's smoking hot tureen.

The hostess at the Lemon Tree was 'old, couthie, courteous Mrs Ronald', who looked after her guests in this 'quiet, cosy howff' in a motherly fashion and fed them on creamy Finnan haddocks and magnificent partan claws. There were also claws of a different kind at the Lemon Tree, for Mrs Ronald kept an eagle in a cage for many years – 'the largest and prettiest specimen I ever saw', said one observer.

The Lemon Tree Inn disappeared when work began on the municipal buildings in 1867, but its memory is kept alive in the old St Catherine's Centre in West North Street, now the new Lemon Tree, a multi-arts centre with a music venue, a theatre and a restaurant. In the same way, the Archibald Simpson will bring a breath of the past to the Castlegate, a reminder of the days when 'the goodly and the godly' wined and dined at the famous New Inn.

23
THE *OSCAR*

It was the first day of April 1813 – April Fool's Day. The early morning was calm and bright, carrying the promise of spring. Five whaling ships were riding at anchor in Aberdeen Bay – the *Hercules*, *Latona*, *Middleton*, *St Andrew* and the *Oscar*. They had taken advantage of a favourable breeze to haul out of the harbour, intending to lie-to outside and wait for the remainder of their crews.

Then, between eight and nine o'clock, Nature played a deadly April Fool's trick on them. The wind changed, snow fell, and a gale began to whip the water, quickly building up to hurricane proportions. The snow became so thick that the men on the ships could scarcely keep their feet. People who remembered that day said that the suddenness and violence of the storm made many townsfolk experience a kind of awe.

There was a curious feeling, a dread almost, that some terrible calamity was about to happen. It was a presentiment, as one local writer put it later, that 'was soon to be fearfully verified'.

A boat from the *Oscar* had gone ashore to pick up some late crew arrivals. By the time it had taken them to the *Oscar*, the whaler was far inshore. The heavy rolling sea and a strong flood tide made it impossible for her to clear Girdleness and she continued to fall to leeward, heading towards the rocky shore. Now the gale unleashed its full fury and about noon the *Oscar* dragged her anchors and went ashore on the rocks at Greyhope.

When the alarm was raised, people from the town crossed the water to Torry by ferry and made for the wreck. There was nothing they could do. They could scarcely see the *Oscar* because of the blinding snow. Helpless, they lined the shore and watched as the vessel broke up and, one by one, the whalermen were swept to their deaths.

On the ship, the crew tried to form a kind of bridge to the nearest high rocks by cutting away the mainmast, but it was hopeless. The fore and mizzen masts fell and men clinging to the rigging dropped like limp dolls and plunged into the sea. The watchers, with only a short distance between them and the wreck, saw men swept off its deck and disappear before their eyes. For a few, safety lay little more than an arm's length away. They had almost struggled ashore when they were swept back by the heavy surf or caught in the wreckage of the ship.

When the forecastle still remained above the water, five men were clinging to it. One was the *Oscar*'s master, Captain John Innes, who was seen making desperate signals for assistance. It was too late – all five were swept away.

One of the men watching on the shore was Captain Richard Jamson, who was the great-grandfather of the minister of St George's-in-the-West Church in Aberdeen. He saw an object floating in the boiling surf and, reaching out with his walking stick, he pulled it ashore. The 'object' was a member of the crew. When he pulled him out of the water he discovered that the man he had saved was his nephew, John Jamson, first mate on the *Oscar*.

Jamson was revived and lived to tell the tale, as did James Venus, a young seamen from Shields. They were the only survivors out of a crew of forty-three men. It was a tragedy that cast a terrible gloom over the city. Apart from the loss of life, the loss of the ship and its equipment was valued at £10,000. Fund-raising events were held for the bereaved, a theatre performance raised £80, and domestic servants in the city 'contributed handsomely'.

Six days after the disaster the *Aberdeen Journal* carried a poem by a local poet, its lines heavy with 'the mournful cry of death and misery'. One verse described the raging sea as 'the messenger of God, charged with His dread decree'. But was the loss of the *Oscar* an act of God? The answer may have lain in one of the verses:

> The gallant ship, prepared to brave
> The northern ocean's mighty wave;
> Her jovial crew, with thoughtless glee,
> Draining the parting cup right merrily.

The 'parting cup' that the whalers drunk was grog, a potent combination of Jamaica rum and water – two parts rum and one part water. Captain Lewis Middleton, an Aberdeen whaling skipper, told in his *Whaling Recollections* how grog was 'served out as regularly as necessary food'. Drunkenness was rife. Whalers often had to lie out in the Bay while saloons on shore were searched for drunken crew members, who were brought alongside in boats and 'hoisted on deck like so many bales of goods'.

It was a fact that the members of the *Oscar*'s crew who arrived late to the ship had been drinking *too* merrily. 'The *Oscar* sailed on the first of April,' wrote Captain Middleton, 'and while waiting in the Bay for the Captain, who was detained on Custom House business, an easterly gale came in from seaward. The crew being drunk were unable to handle the ship. She was driven ashore on the Girdleness, became a total wreck, and only the First Mate and one boy were saved.'

The Greyhope disaster, bad as it was, could have been worse. Both the *St Andrew* and the *Hercules* were riding within a short distance of the *Oscar*. It was regarded as something of a miracle that they escaped the same fate. The *Latona* also went unscathed in that April Fool's Day storm, but later in the year it was struck by ice in the Davis Straits and went down in fifteen minutes.

Two years later, history repeated itself at Greyhope Bay. On January 26, 1815, the brig *Caledonia* foundered in a storm at the mouth of the harbour and her crew of seven were all drowned, while the schooner *Providence*, seeking safety from the storm, was wrecked with the loss of her crew. The trading smack *Thames* was driven to the rocks almost at the same spot that the *Oscar* had been wrecked. Her crew and passengers – nine people in all – were drowned.

From Torry Hill, you can look down through the houses and catch glimpses of the harbour and Greyhope Bay. Two of the streets have names that span the years to those far-off whaling days. They are called Oscar Road and Oscar Place.

24

THE GHAIST'S RAW

Aberdeen lost a street with a rich and prosperous history when the planners and builders got to work clearing the Guestrow. Today, only a token strip of land bordering Broad Street shows that it ever existed. 'A name unique to Aberdeen,' says a plaque on the wall, 'but its origin is obscure.'

The Guestrow originally ran from the Netherkirkgate to the Upperkirkgate. A number of the city's Provosts lived there, including Sir George Skene, who built Skene House, where the Duke of Cumberland stayed in 1746. Today it is a period domestic museum. The variety of businesses in the street was said to be 'quite remarkable' . . . bakers, tailors, corkcutters, clockmakers, wrights, slaters, boarding-house keepers, dentists, musical instrument makers. For a time, there was also a Burking House in the street (see Chapter 9).

Provost Skene's house. The oldest house in the Guestrow.

All that is left of the Guestrow.

How did the Guestrow get its name? People have argued over this question for years. Some say it was from the celebrities who once stayed there – the guests in Guestrow – others that it had a more macabre origin. It came, not from guests, but from ghosts. In fact, old records show it as the Ghaist Raw.

The Guestrow's neighbouring street, Broad Street, or the Broadgate as it was called, seems to be too narrow to carry such a name. Yet at one time, when there were no buildings between Broad Street and Greyfriars Kirk, the Broadgate 'was of great breadth and appropriately named'.

That ended some three centuries ago when, according to the New Statistical Account of 1845, a double row of houses was built down the middle of the Broadgate. This reduced the street 'from about 35 paces to its present breadth of about 15 or 18 paces, and the west side of it, known by the name of the Guestrow, became a separate street'. The NSA was accurate enough; I paced it out and the measurment was exactly 18 paces.

There have been different accounts of how these changes took place, just as there are different theories on the name. William Kennedy, in his *Annals of Aberdeen,* said that 'strangers of respectability' were often housed there, 'hence the name of Guestraw'. One visitor, the

Rev. James Hall, from London, who was impressed by the hospitality of Aberdonians, stayed 'in the street called the Guest's Row'.

These views have been discounted – and in come the ghosties. The Guestrow stood on high ground overlooking St Nicholas churchyard. There were no houses between it and the kirkyard, as there are now, and it was said that from the Guestrow the ghosts of the dead could be seen on their nightly walks in the area. So it became the Ghaist Raw.

Turn back the pages of history to the 16th and 17th centuries and the argument seems to be clinched. Charters of that time show that the Guestrow was set down as *Vicus Lemurum* – the Road of the Spirits.

25
FLEEIN' GEORDIE

Fleein' Geordie never found his proper niche in the history of manned flight. He was the son of Patrick Davidson, a partner in a prominent Aberdeen law firm, and for a time it seemed as if he might rank alongside the pioneers of the air, men like A.V. Roe and the Wright brothers. But it didn't quite work out that way . . .

George Louis Outram Davidson was a dreamer, a man obsessed by a Tennyson poem which saw a vision of a world in which 'argosies of magic sails' filled the skies:

> Saw the heavens fill with commerce,
> argosies of magic sails,
> Pilots of the purple twilight
> dropping down with costly bales.

Davidson visualised himself having a major role in that great leap into the future – by becoming the first 'Birdman'. Long after he had made his bid for aerial fame he recalled how the dream had first formed in his mind. 'Fifty-three years ago', he told a farmer near his home at Inchmarlo, Banchory, in 1932, 'I was lying on my back here looking up at the sky and watching the birds and thinking that man should be able to do the same thing.'

Davidson's father, Patrick, carried on his legal business in Aberdeen but lived on an estate near Banchory, a quiet Deeside village which is now part of the city's commuter belt. It was there – at Inchmarlo Cottage, on the outskirts of Banchory – that Fleein' Geordie made plans to launch himself into the air – and into the history books.

'If we wish to attain real flight', he wrote, 'we must design a flying machine in which mechanical rotary wings shall be substituted for and do the same work as the reciprocal wings of the birds'. He had no time for the 'run and jump' brigade – people who thought they could get results 'with a run or a jump and a flimsy structure of bamboo.'

His closest rival, Percy Pilcher, who was known as the Birdman of Cardross, was one of the 'run and jump' school, as was the German flier Otto Lilienthal. 'These gentlemen', said Davidson, 'have to

George Louis Outram Davidson.

trundle their machines up to the top of a hill before they begin to glide.' Lilienthal was killed in a glider crash in 1896.

Davidson's first experiments with flight involved model gliders. An article by him on 'Practical Mechanical Flight' was illustrated by a photograph captioned 'G.L.O. Davidson's Toy Glider'. It showed a bat-like structure over the woods at Inchmarlo in 1897. Curiously enough, Percy Pilcher's first glider, completed two years earlier, was called the Bat, and his fourth glider, the Hawk, built in 1896, also looked like a bat in flight.

Andrew Noble, a photographer in the town from 1890 to 1929, had a picture of a large-scale model of a flying machine made by Davidson; probably the 'toy glider' seen over the Inchmarlo woods. It was a curious contraption, standing on four spiky legs, looking like a UFO from outer space. Fleein' Geordie, wearing a bonnet and bow-tie, stood beside it, a roll of cord or string sticking from his pocket.

The toy glider must have passed its test, for later that year a full-size machine was built and ready for flight. Like Pilcher's glider, it looked clumsy – 'very unwieldy, too heavy to fly', was the verdict of local folk. The Banchory author, V.J. Buchan Watt, writing in 1947, said it was 'a machine made of wood which had affixed at the sides "wings" which flapped up and down when operated by someone in the machine, rowing as in a boat'.

All Banchory was agog on the day of the trial flight. Crowds gathered in the Burnett Park, where the flight was to take place, the machine hurling itself into the air on a given signal. 'At last the signal came,' wrote Buchan Watt. 'Cameras clicked as the strange machine rose into the air and crashed to the ground. The "pilot" was unhurt, but the machine was badly damaged. Thus ended the attempt to conquer the air.'

Time has dimmed the details of the attempt to fly like a bird. Different versions of what happened have drifted down the years . . . that the aircraft was built on a platform and fell to the ground when it took off; that it flapped its wings, half rose into the air and collapsed; and that it actually rose a few yards from the ground.

Fleein' Geordie may have failed to soar into the skies, but Tennyson's vision of 'argosies of magic sails' remained in his mind. The following year he went to England to build a high-wing monoplane which the prospectus called 'Davidson's Air Car'. Others called it 'Davidson's Folly'. It had a 100-feet span, with an enclosed fuselage seating twenty passengers along its 45-feet length. The upward thrust was obtained by two large rotary lifters, or 'gyropters', as Davidson called them. The power came from two 50 h.p. Stanley steam-car engines. The machine weighed over 7.5 tons.

Davidson, who was a founder member of the Royal Aeronautical Society, presented a paper to the society in which he said that many people thought he should attempt a flight in his machine 'from the top of St Paul's or the Eiffel'. They believed that the correct way to start his first flying machine was from a height, but Davidson, still nursing contempt for the 'run and jump' brigade, said firmly, 'I'll start my Air Car from the level of the ground.'

Fleein' Geordie's visions of the future were no less imaginative that the poet Tennyson's. He, too, 'dipt into the future, far as human eye could see', and predicted a time when people would 'take the 12 o'clock Car to Manchester, arrive in good time for one o'clock lunch, stay for afternoon tea, and get back to London for dinner'. He visualised large air depots being established. In crowded cities these might take the form of enormous platforms; he drew a sketch of how one would look in the heart of London.

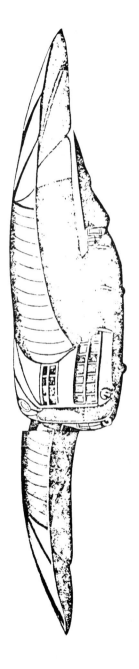

A sketch of Davidson's proposed 'Air Car', which some people called 'Davidson's Folly'.

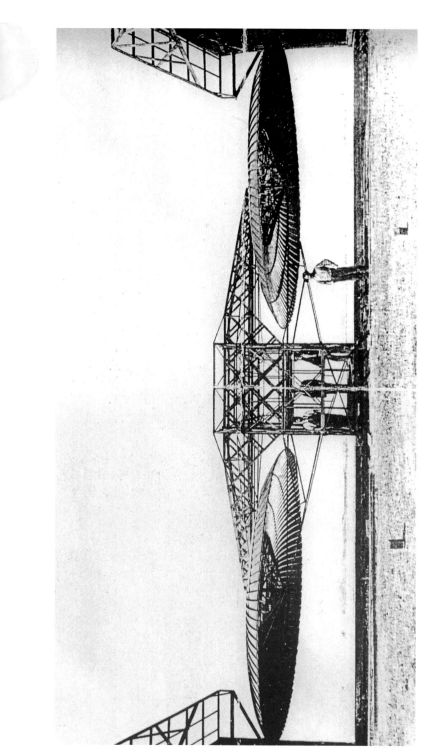

Davidson's flying machine in course of construction at Montclair, Colorado, USA in October 1907.

But he also had a grimmer vision of the age of flight. 'The main object of flying machines', he said, 'will be to enable us to drop dynamite on our enemies.'

Nothing came of his Air Car plan, but in 1906 Davidson produced a revised design and went off to build it in America. In the early days he employed A.V. Roe (later to found the Avro aircraft company) as a draughtsman at his offices in London. The 1906 version was never completed, but Davidson claimed that it proved that a heavy machine could lift itself into the air with rotary wings.

In 1907 he produced a prospectus for a machine he called the 'Gyropter', which would carry 20 passengers and have a speed of 200 m.p.h. Between January 1910 and March 1911, more than 650 people visited the works at Taplow in Buckinghamshire to watch it being built. But history repeated itself; the money ran out and Davidson had another failure on his hands.

Davidson had private means, but over the years he had poured £15,000 of it down the drain in his obsession with flight. His family motto might well have been the gloomy comment of a leading flight magazine: 'Nothing teaches so much as failure.' It taught Davidson that it was time to disappear from the public eye, for nothing more was heard of him until 1929, when the first non-stop flight from Britain to India was completed. He re-emerged then to declare that the gyropter or, helicopter, was the flying machine of the future. He died at Inchmarlo in June 1939.

The names of the pioneers of flight, men like the Wright brothers, Pilcher, Avro and Lilienthal, have gone into the history books, but Davidson has been ignored, although much of what he prophesied has come to pass. He died within months of a war that saw aircraft 'dropping dynamite from the clouds', and if he had lived on he would have seen great 'air depots' springing up all over the country. He would also have seen his 'gyropters', the helicopters of today, dropping in and out of Aberdeen's 'air depot', upholding his long-held belief in the principle of direct-lift in flight.

But Fleein' Geordie might have had a wry smile at the spectacle of hang-gliders dropping like butterflies from launch points along the Dee valley. The 'run and jump' brigade are still with us . . .

26
PEACOCK'S FEATHERS

Although Aberdeen has produced a string of well-known dancing teachers over the years, none has ever achieved the heights reached by Francis Peacock. He was the man who had a Castlegate close named after him . . . the man who made even the Civic Fathers dance to his tune.

When he was at the height of his fame, he wrote a pamphlet called 'Peacock on Dancing'. The city magistrates decided that the councillors should learn to 'trip the light fantastic' and ordered twenty copies of it. The whole town rocked with laughter at the idea of the Lord Provost and baillies twirling about on a dance floor and ending up on their doups. William Walker, author of *The Bards of Bon-Accord,* wrote about 'the grotesquely comical idea of our "bailie bodies", in all their weight of wisdom, taking to the business of "the light fantastic toe".' In his book he published a satirical poem on the topic, written by some anonymous versifier. It went like this:

> God prosper long our Lord Provost,
> Town Clerk an' Bailies a';
> An grant that in their reelin' fits,
> Doup-scud* they winna fa.

> For they hae coff'd a score o' buiks,
> On dancing ilka ane;
> Though folk in sober guise wad trow
> Their dancin' days were dane.

> Now bob for bob an' loup for loup
> Fornent the Cha'mer door;
> Grave magistrates will rax their legs,
> Fan their sederunt's o'er.

> Ere twa three bouts, their win' will fag,
> An' puffin' come instead;
> Nae wonder they'll be soon dane out,
> For dancin's nae their trade.

*Fall heavily on the buttocks.

Our city fathers were not always so enthusiastic about dancing. In 1695, the town council prohibited a dancing master called Mr Batham from 'haveing any publict balls of dancing in this place'. They must have changed their minds, for William Kennedy, in his *Annals of Aberdeen*, said that dancing was introduced to Aberdeen about the beginning of the 18th century 'to teach the young citizens manners and good breeding'.

But it had a slow start. In 1742 a number of top people in the city complained to the Town Council 'that the town was at great loss for want of a right dancing master to educate their children'. The Council advertised the post and two candidates, James Stuart of Montrose, and William Troup of Aberdeen, were asked to show their paces. They did so in the Trinity Hall in front of the magistrates and a 'great number of gentlemen and ladys'.

James Stuart was chosen, but he had a short reign. Whether or not he was too fond of the bottle, or engaged in more intimate pleasures, will never be known, but in 1746 the Council advertised again for a dancing master 'of a sober, discreet, and moral character'. Enter Francis Peacock, from Edinburgh, who was appointed sole dancing master in the burgh. The Council added the solemn qualification that he would hold the post 'during his good behaviour'.

Peacock, who was allowed 'to take seven shillings sterling monthly for each scholar, besides payment for the musick', was twenty-three when he came to Aberdeen. He quickly spread his feathers, marrying an Aberdeen girl, Ellen Forbes (they had their first daughter in 1749), and setting himself up as the city's new dancing master. His first dancing school was a building in the Castlegate, but when it was about to be demolished for the making of Marischal Street he moved to premises in Mealmarket Street.

His next move was back to a house in the Castlegate known as Skipper Scott's tavern, where the Old Pretender dined when passing through Aberdeen in 1715. The old inn was in one of the many closes that riddled the Castlegate. The city's new dancing master built several houses in the alley, which was to become known to generations of Aberdonians as Peacock's Close.

Aberdeen has always been a musical city. Back through the centuries, and right up to the present day, music has had the backing of the local council. In 1662, one writer was so carried away by it that he described our civic leaders as 'their honourable wisdoms the Lord

Provost, Baillies, and Town Council – a harmonious concert of as many musicians as Magistrates'.

The city's musical development was boosted by an association founded in 1748 – the Aberdeen Musical Society. Francis Peacock was one of the principal members of the society, which had in its ranks top people from both town and county . . . provosts and professors, earls and lairds, barons and baronets, colonels, merchants and artists. It gave weekly public concerts for many years and was wound up in 1838.

In 1761, the society played a major role in celebrations marking the Coronation of King George III. Peacock composed the music for 'an anthem' performed in the Marischal College Hall, and afterwards they marched to the Castlegate. The Broadgate trembled to the blast and brrumph of the 'drums, pipes and French horns of the Gentlemen of the Musical Society' as they led a 'boisterous processon to the Market Cross to drink the health of the King and other members of the Royal Family'.

Peacock was an artist as well as a musician and a dancer. He painted miniatures which were well thought of at the time. In 1762 he published a book, *Fifty Favourite Scotch Airs for the Violin,* and when he was over eighty years of age he published another, *Sketches Relative to Dancing.* Old age placed no restrictions on him. He often played host to Aberdeen's leading citizens in his house in Peacock's Close, and when he was on the edge of becoming an octogenarian he held balls which started at four o'clock in the afternoon and often continued till four o'clock next morning.

Peacock built a yellow, stucco-covered house for himself in the Fountainhall area of the city and called it Villa Franca. It was demolished to make way for Hamilton Place West and No. 156 now stands on the site.

Francis Peacock died on June 26, 1807, in his 84th year. He had danced his way into the affections of the townsfolk and he left money to be distributed to various institutions in the city after his death. In 1814 the Town Council gave permission for a tablet to be erected to his memory in Drum's Aisle in St Nicholas Church on payment of five guineas, but the tablet was never put up. No one knows what happened to it.

There is, however, the kind of memorial that he might have liked best – the sign that says Peacock Close in the Castlegate. When the dancing master lived in Skipper Scott's old tavern, the close was

The Peacock Printmaker's shop in the Castlegate, with closes on each side of it. It has now changed hands.

a place of some distinction, but after his death it became tawdry and disreputable, a slum alley like Sinclair's Close, the Cowgate and Mauchline Tower Court, which have all gone. G.M. Fraser, Aberdeen's librarian, wrote in his book, *Aberdeen Street Names*, that Peacock Close once had an evil name among the streets of the town.

In 1850, the feuars and proprietors asked the police commissioners of Aberdeen to change the name of the close. It had, they said, 'fallen into such disrepute that the very name was sufficient to deter many respectable parties from taking houses in that quarter'. The Board, perhaps because of the role Francis Peacock had played in the life of the city, refused to make the change.

G.M. Fraser said in 1911 that the close would soon be a thing of the past. 'The old crowded tenements are nearly all abandoned,' he wrote, 'and the properties will in due time be pulled down. The oldest house has had some interesting features in its day. It had the distinction of a flag-staff, and an underground passage, not to speak of the oak-panelling of its rooms. Even historical interest can not regret the clearance that must soon obliterate a street name that has continued the memory of this most worthy citizen to our own day.'

The Peacock Printmakers workshop, with a peacock symbol above the door.

Eighty-six years later, Peacock Close survives. There is a plaque at the entrance recording Francis Peacock's connection with it, but it is a gloomy, uninviting alley. The Castlegate story is a fascinating one. Much of the city's history has its roots there, and when I wrote *The Granite City* in 1988 I suggested that, when it was restored, a museum might be built behind one of its old closes, perhaps alongside the Peacock Printers, next to Peacock Close, where there is a print musueum almost on the spot where Edward Raban produced his first *Aberdeen Almanac*.

The Castlegate has been smartened up and pedestrianised, but there is still little to show that this was once the heartbeat of the city. God prosper our Lord Provost, Town Clerk an' Bailies a' . . . maybe they will set it right in their own good time.

27

RIDING THE STANG

I kenna what we wives wad dee
Wi'carls that drink and bang,
But for the halesome discipline
O' ryding o' the stange.

The curious verse above comes from a poem written three centuries ago by an unknown Huntly poet. It tells what happened in the Strathbogie town in 1734, when a local tailor, John Fraser, took to drink and began to beat his wife, Anne Johnstone. Time and again he abused her and finally her neighbours decided to do something about it. They made him 'ride the stang'.

The ancient ritual of riding the stang goes far back in time. It was a punishment inflicted only on married people. If a husband abused his wife, or if a wife hen-pecked her husband, or if either proved unfaithful to the other, the offender was made to undergo the ordeal. The stang was a wooden pole, carried upon men's shoulders. The delinquent was mounted on it and carried from place to place, while a noisy throng jeered and mocked the sufferer.

It appeared that hen-pecked husbands were also liable to the punishment for *allowing* themselves to come too much under petticoat government. This was shown in a verse which went –

Like hen-pick'd husbands riding the stang,
He by the mane on tail and knees hang,
Attended with a mighty noise
Of knaves and fools and boys.

Noise was important. Men, women and children in a village would come to the riding of the stang, armed with instruments to create a hullabaloo – horns, frying pans and tea kettles, iron pots with lids used as cymbals, fire shovels and tongs and tin and wooden pails drummed on with pieces of iron.

Before the victim mounted the stang his misdeeds were proclaimed by a herald. The following is a rhyming proclamation made on the case of a wife-beater:

Ran, tan, tan; ran, tan, ran,
To the sound of this pan;
This is to give notice that Tom Trotter
Has beaten his good woman!
For what and for why?
'Cause she ate when she was hungry,
And drank when she was dry.
Ran, tan, ran, tan, tan,
Hurrah – hurrah! For this good woman!
He beat her, he beat her, he beat her indeed,
For spending a penny when she had need.
He beat her black, he beat her blue;
When Old Nick gets him, he'll give him his due;
Ran, tan tan; ran, tan, tan;
We'll send him there in this old frying pan.

Not all the wife-beating husbands who rode the stang took their punishment meekly. The women who put John Fraser, the Huntly tailor, on the stang thought that their action was perfectly legal, but Fraser lodged a charge against them. Their response was to draw up a 'Petition to the Bailie of the Regality of Huntly for a toleration to the stang (AD 1734)'.

The petition pointed out that they meant only to frighten the tailor. At the same time, the petitioners asked for permission for the continued use of the 'stang' or some 'more prudent method', pleading that they must have some means of retaliation to prevent their husbands ill-treating them.

The petition read:

Upon the eleventh of January instant, the said John Fraser did, under cloud of night, most inhumanly and barbarously beat and bruise Anne Johnston, his said spouse, to the effusion of her blood and great hazard and peril of her life. And not only that, but it is his constant practice, as can be attested by severalls of the neighbourhood, who have divers and sundry times risen from their beds at mid-night, and has rescued her out of his merciless hands, or she had been most miserably butchered by him.

And seeing your petitioners are informed that the said Fraser has given ane information to your Lordships against some of our good neighbours who, upon Saturday last, being the twelfth instant, went to his house alledging they would cause him Ride the Stang (use and wont in such cases) but to our certain knowledge with no other design than to fright and deter him from his villanous and cruell usage of his said spouse in all time coming.

In seeking a decision granting 'a toleration to the Stang', the petitioners said that the stang was 'not only practicable to this place, but in most pairts of this kingdome, being, we know, no Act of Parliament to the contrair.' Failing a decision on 'toleration', they requested their Lordships to give their opinion on how to prevent 'more fatall consequences, otherwise we must expect to fall victims to our husbands' displeasure'. There were eleven signatories to the petition.

When the case came to trial the women acknowledged that they took part in 'the cryme labelled', and admitted that they attacked Fraser 'in the face of the sun, about three in the afternoon, tore his clothes and abused his person, by carrying him in a publick manner through the toun of Huntly upon a tree'. The baillie found them guilty and ordered each of them to 'pay five pounds sterling, in name of damages to the private party'.

The women had the backing of their menfolk when they gave John Fraser his come-uppance, but there were no men's names in the petition, One verse in 'The Riding of the Stange' mentioned 'the mob o' loons and kimmers', A 'kimmer' was a married woman. It was a woman, Betty Burgie, who told the tale of what happened at the riding of the stang:

> Draw in about the creepie, Jean,
> Sit doon, sirs, ane and a',
> And I'll tell the story head and tail!
> And hoo it did befa'!

> Yon useless brat, the Tailour carl,
> began to ding his wife,
> And twa-three o' the neighbours roun'
> Has halflins ta'en his life.

> 'Whisht! Whisht!' cried Jamie Meldrum,
> 'Just hear that waesome mane –
> That Devil's-buckie, Fraser,
> He's thrashin's wife again.

> 'There's no an 'ook in a' the year
> But he gangs on the spree,
> And then his wee bit wifikie
> Maun a' his anger dree.'

Johnie Falconer said that the Tailor was 'fit to bring black disgrace upon our toon', and Sandy Brown declared that they should seize the cowardly carl and 'gar him ride the stange'. 'Half a hunner' men ran to get a sapling from the wood and then they went for Fraser.

> They trail'd the Tailor frae his cloots,
> And set him on the stange,
> And aye they rode him up an' doon
> Amo' the motley thrang.
>
> And aye the kimmers leugh and cried,
> 'Hech, gi'emt rough and strang;
> There's nae an Act o' Parliament
> Gainst ryding o' the stange.
> The Tailor like a trooper swore
>
> He'd bang them at the law,
> But the mob o' loons and kimmers
> Gae the tither great guffaw.
> They rode him by the stan'in stanes,
>
> And round the very kirk,
> And aye the Tailor's hurdies
> Got the tither waesome jerk.
> And how they gar'd him hodge and jump
>
> Upon the jaggit pole,
> I'm sure 'twas mair than rumple bane
> O' mortal man cud thole.
> Wi' shout and cry they bare him by
>
> The cordiwaner's sta',
> But case it sud be his turn neist,
> Faith! Cordy slunk awa'.
> At length and lang frae aff the stange
>
> The Tailor lap by force,
> And hirpled to his cloots again.
> Just like a spavied horse.
>
> I've lived in Huntly, wife and bairn,
> Twa' score o' years and mae,
> But never got I half the fun
> That I hae got the day.

There have been various references in literature to the practice, both in prose and verse. The Edinburgh poet Allan Ramsay wrote about 'a caber rough' being mounted when a woman 'rade the stang', so it seems as if was well-known in Auld Reekie. At Dalkeith, in

1809, it was reported that 'a mob exercised authority in its own style, making loose women ride the Stang'.

In 1824, Riding the Stang was described as 'a public punishment inflicted on adulterers and fornicators. A large pole is got and passed between the culprit's legs; he is then carried and cudgelled through the *clauchan*'. Lines from a verse in 1857 said:

> Ye gallop the stang,
> Till your hurdies are nicket.

The *Caledonian Mercury* carried a paragraph about a George Porteous, a blacksmith, who 'having severely beaten and bruised his wife, thought himself so highly affronted by the neighbours riding the stang for him, that, taking remorse, he went and hanged himself the day after'.

The stang was used for less painful purposes than punishng wife-beaters. It was also said to be the shaft of a cart, or part of an Orkney plough. In *Scottish Notes and Queries* in 1933 there was a reference to 'a new stang for the bell . . . 2s 6d' and a report in the Aberdeen burgh records in 1726 noted that 'the stang of the tolbooth weather cock was loose'.

Oddly enough, the word 'stang' was used to describe a person who was a 'live-wire', the life and soul of a party. The poem *Whistle-Binkie* carried the lines:

> Baith bodies toil'd to mak' gowd
> in a lump,
> But Maggie was counted the
> Stang o' the trump.

Riding the stang was very much in use in the days when punishments were calculated to hold delinquents up to public ridicule and shame. This was done with the pillory, the ducking stool, the drunkard's cloak, the whirligig, and others, but the one that lingered on longest was the stang. Robert Chambers said that to his certain knowledge it was inflicted as late as October 1862.

What would wives do without this 'halesome discipline?' the poem asked. Well, wife beating is no doubt just as prevalent today as it was a few centuries ago. 'Carls that drink' still knock their wives about, and hen-pecked husbands still get hot tongue from shrewish partners. Maybe the stang will make a comeback!

28
THE PIRATES

It was said to be like a Gilbert and Sullivan opera . . . piracy on the high seas off the coast of Aberdeen. It happened in 1971 when the crew of the 106-feet-long Aberdeen trawler, the *Mary Craig*, hi-jacked the vessel, destroyed the ship's log book, took possession of the bonded stores, and dumped the skipper and four crewmen at the Buchan port of Peterhead.

The skipper telephoned his office in Aberdeen and the police and Royal Navy were alerted. Meanwhile, the *Mary Craig* zig-zagged out to sea like a drunken sailor pursued by several trawlers and other vessels.

In retrospect, it was a hilarious episode that the flamboyant lawyer Nicholas Fairbarn, defending one of the 'pirates', described as 'a source of innocent merriment'. But, shiver-me-timbers, the grave-faced judge, Lord Cameron, sitting in judgement in the High Court at Aberdeen, didn't think it funny.

There was a 'Yo! Ho! Ho! and a bottle of Rum' atmosphere about the whole thing – or, at any rate, Yo! Ho! Ho! and 96 cans of beer, for that was what was missing from the ship's bondage stores when the trawler finally returned to port. The pattern for the whole affair was set on October 8 when the *Mary Craig* sailed from Aberdeen. It returned the same day because the cook was drunk and unfit for duty.

The *Mary Craig* was on its way to the West Coast fishing grounds when five members of the crew took 'masterful possession' of it. They were eight or nine miles from Aberdeen when the men told Skipper Colin Cordiner they were hi-jacking the ship. When he pointed out that they were doing wrong they told him to shut up – and locked him in his cabin.

Released a short time later, he suggested to the mutineers that they should go to their beds and sleep it off. 'They all had a good drink,' he said. They didn't take his advice, but they had no idea where to go. Skipper Cordiner told them that with their lack of navigation they should head east. After he was landed at Peterhead, the trawler *Coastal Empress* was contacted and told to shadow the 'runaway' vessel.

The *Mary Craig*, according to charges that were eventually dropped, tried to ram the *Coastal Empress*. This happened when the

Coastal Empress found the 'pirate' ship forty miles off the Buchan coast. Its engines had stopped, and it was being battered by a gale. The subdued 'pirates' acepted a tow line and twenty-four hours after leaving Aberdeen the *Mary Craig* was escorted into port by the *Coastal Empress* and the tug *Sea Griffon*.

The five men – Alexander Cameron, William Massie, Colin Charles, Ronald Park and Andrew Innes – were tried at the High Court in Aberdeen. It was the first case of its kind in Scotland since the abolition of the High Court of Admiralty more than a century and a half earlier. The charge was 'taking masterful posession of the *Mary Craig*' – the word 'piracy' was never used. But there was a good deal of discussion over whether or not the accused men had actually committed piracy. The irrepressible Fairbairn thought not. 'Was Massie a pirate,' he asked, 'when he went downstairs and told the chief engineer he was taking over, the chief engineer told him to get lost – and he got lost.'

Mr Fairbairn enlisted Gilbert and Sullivan to back his argument. Skipper Cordiner's departure from the *Mary Craig*, he said, was like a line from the *Pirates of Penzance*, and he quoted: 'We yield at once with humbled mien, because with all our faults we love our Queen.' Mr Gavin Young, defending the three other men, said it was 'a drunken prank which rather misfired'.

Nevertheless, the men were found guilty and sent to jail – Cameron for thirteen months, Massie for eighteen months, Charles for two years, Park for two years and Innes for eighteen months. An appeal against the sentences was dismissed by the Court of Criminal Appeal in Edinburgh.

So that was the end of a curious affair which brought shades of Captain Bluebeard and Long John Silver to the streets of Aberdeen. Today it is largely forgotten, but if events had taken a different turn the *Mary Craig* might still be in the news. In 1994, more than twenty years after the piracy incident, the owners of the trawler offered it to the town as a heritage exhibit. The cost of putting the trawler on a dry berth in a Maritime Heritage Park at Footdee would have been at least £460,000. The city's councillors, canny Aberdonians that they were, turned the offer down.

For a time the old trawler operated as an oil-rig stand-by vessel and in 1992 it was berthed at Dundee. But the old tub hadn't given up her roaming. At 7.40 a.m. on 27 November 1994, she sailed from Aberdeen, bound for London. The last that was heard of her was that she was still operating as a stand-by safety vessel.

29

THE HORSESHOE

When ships entering Aberdeen harbour come bouncing down the navigation channel, they pass the remains of an old jetty known to Fittie folk as the Horseshoe. It was built three centuries ago on the north side of the channel to protect shipping entering the harbour, but it became a hazard, not a help, and most of it was removed.

Two other quaintly-named jetties can be seen on the south side of the channel. One is called the Banana Jetty, because of its shape, and the other is a moss-encrusted pier called the Skate's Nose.

The 'U' of the Horseshoe lies just below the Round House. It is the better-known jetty, for it was planned by the famous Yorkshire engineer John Smeaton, who designed the North Pier. The pier, built in 1781, was a notable achievement, but after it was completed a major snag was discovered – heavy easterly swells racing up the channel damaged the pier and became a danger to shipping.

Smeaton was called back to solve the problem. He thought the solution was to build a jetty projecting from the pier into the channel – a 'catch pier'. It was 50 yards long, pointing inwards to divert waves from the north side of the channel and to prevent them entering the harbour.

At first, the jetty was called Smeaton's Jetty, but it was later renamed in honour of the city's Provost and carried the inscription *Jno* (John) *Abercrombie Provost 1789*. By 1820 it had become an obstruction to shipping. It also interfered with the dredging of the channel, so most of it was removed. About 60 feet of it was left – for a special reason.

Before steam tugs came into use, ships had great difficulty getting up the channel when there was a strong breeze against them. The only way to get them into harbour was to have men pulling them in with ropes. So, when the wind was in the west, ships were hauled into the harbour by ropes wrapped around a capstan on what remained of the Abercrombie Jetty.

The capstan is still there – and if it could speak it would tell a terrible story. In the first half of the 19th century no fewer than five vessels were wrecked while attempting to enter the channel. The first

The Horseshoe.

was the *Ossian* in 1822, two years after the Horseshoe was demolished, the next the *Grampian* in 1830, followed by the *Brilliant* in 1839 and the *Velocity* in 1848. In 1853 came the worst disaster of all – the sinking of the *Duke of Sutherland*, an iron paddle steamer from London.

The *Brilliant* was one of the regular trading steamers that operated between Leith and Aberdeen. Its last voyage took place on Thursday 12 December, 1839. On its way north it had been battered by a hurricane during the night, but it reached Aberdeen Bay in the early morning. Between five and six o'clock it was struck by a huge wave north of Girdleness. The commander, Captain Wade, was swept overboard and the mate took charge, but a succession of heavy seas carried the vessel on to the North Pier. There was a rush for the fore quarter deck and passengers and crew were safely landed, but one passenger had his leg broken.

A woman with four children left two in the cabin until she got the others ashore. When that was done she ran back for the remaining two youngsters, who were also safely landed. Before she could follow them the *Brilliant* broke away from the pier, leaving her, along with the cook and second engineer, on board the stricken ship. The two men fastened a line round the woman's waist and threw the other end to survivors on the shore. She was then pulled on to dry land and reunited with her children.

The Horseshoe and Round House.

The ship caught fire, but the cargo was saved from the wreck, although some of it was badly damaged. Eventually, the ship broke up and her wreckage was scattered along the shore. It was a sad end for the *Brilliant*, which had eighteen year's service behind it – and no accidents.

The *Duke of Sutherland* was wrecked on April Fool's Day 1853. It had sailed from London on 31 March, with twenty-five passengers and a crew of thirty on board, as well as general cargo. There were high winds and heavy rain when she reached Aberdeen and the master, Captain Edward Howling, had to wait for permission to enter the harbour.

The steamer was making good headway when it was struck by a heavy sea, then a second sea broke over her and threw her on to the shelving rocks at the breakwater. Captain Howling gave orders to launch the lifeboats. Female passengers were clinging to the rails or spars and almost every sea carried them out of the arms of those leading them to the boat. Only seven men and a woman got into the first boat. They were landed in safety.

A lifeboat was launched, but it was badly damaged in getting alongside the steamer and only thirteen men and two women got on to her and were landed on the beach. Six men manned a salmon cobble and put off to the wreck, but the boat capsized and five of the crew were drowned. Only one man got ashore safely.

The hero of the disaster was the steamer's chief steward, Duncan Christie. He helped to get fifteen passengers into a boat, then caught a rocket-line and hauled it in with his own hands. He saved nineteen lives and was the last to leave the vessel.

The sixteen people drowned included Captain Howling. Among them was a Mr Burgess, who was returning home from the Australian gold diggings. A belt with nearly £50 in it was found on his body later. Another victim was a Miss Sophia Catherine Bremner, who was returning to Aberdeen to marry a prominent member of the legal profession. She had her bride's cake and marriage trousseau on board and her lover was anxiously waiting for her on the pier.

The *Duke of Sutherland* was an iron steamer built on the Clyde in 1847 at a cost of about £28,000. The cargo was estimated at a value of £8,000.

When the *Brilliant* was wrecked a party of soldiers of the 91st regiment, who were stationed in the city, were marched to the spot to 'preserve order', in other words, to ensure that nobody helped themselves to cargo that was washed ashore. It was a different story when the *Duke of Sutherland* was wrecked. Although a watch was kept, a number of people got away with 'great hauls of goods'. Long before darkness had fallen, the beach was strewn with paraphernalia from the ship. There were drapery goods of every description, including parasols galore for the summer season – one draper lost £750 worth, another £250 – and huge quantities of cheese, oranges and other foods.

People descended onto the beach like vultures, grabbing what they could lay their hands on. The military were called out and formed a cordon along the beach. Fires were lit, but despite all the precautions huge quantities of articles were carried ashore. Some were hidden in sandbanks. In many cases the thieves couldn't find the hiding places and for years afterwards bundles of decayed ribbons, umbrellas and parasol frames were found in the sand.

30

MARKET CROSS

Aberdeen's ancient Market Cross, now little more than a historical curiosity in the Castlegate, was once the focal point of city life. People gathered there to hear proclamations, watch executions and celebrate coronations. Fishwives sat on its steps selling partans and 'haddies', while other vendors did a brisk trade in sweetmeats, boot laces and ballads.

But, strangest of all, the old Cross, with its six open arches crowned by panelled portraits of ten Stuart sovereigns, was for a short time Aberdeen's main post office.

In 1821, when the Cross was found to be so badly in need of repair that it had to be taken down and rebuilt, the Town Council decided to 'convert the interior into a shop' to provide more civic revenue. Four hucksters' booths were removed from inside the arches and 'a sort of shop' was made.

The arches were boarded up and converted into an entrance door and windows and in April, 1822, Aberdeen's new Post Office opened up for business. The postmaster, Alexander Dingwall, paid £25 a year in rent, and as G.M. Fraser, the city librarian, commented in later years, 'A new era seemed to be opening in its long and interesting history.'

The new era was short-lived. The Post Office lasted only into the following year, when it moved to premises in Union Street. It may be that Mr Dingwall decided that claustrophobia was too high a price to pay for a cheap rent. The 'compartment', as it was called, then became a coaching office, and it was from there that the famous coach 'The Defiance' set out on its journeys to Edinburgh.

William Robbie wrote about the Market Cross in his *Aberdeen: Its Traditions and History* in 1893.

> The incidents that have taken place at and around the Cross are innumerable and of all kinds – grave and gay, melancholy and mirthful. On occasions of public rejoicing it was around the Cross that the people gathered to give expression to their loyalty, as well as to partake of the good cheer frequently provided for their entertainment.

The Mercat Cross in the Castlegate.

There was plenty of gaiety when Queen Margaret visited the city in 1511 – and no lack of good cheer. The poet William Dunbar wrote:

> At hir cumming great was the mirth and joy,
> For at thar Croce aboundantlie ran wyne.

Carping about the Common Good Fund today pales into insignificance when you learn that at the coronation of Charles II no less than 'twa punsheoners of wyne, with spycerie in great abundance' was handed out at the Market Cross of Aberdeen. A puncheon is a large cask, usually holding between 70 and 120 gallons, which means that Aberdonians celebrated Charles's coronation with about 240 gallons of wine.

But it wasn't all fun and games around the Cross. It was there that punishment was handed out to wrongdoers – whipping, branding on the cheek with a hot iron, and standing in the pillory or in the branks – a sort of iron gag used to silence female scolds. In 1583, two people convicted of adultery were sentenced to be bound and exposed at the Market Cross for three hours and after that to be burned with a hot iron on their cheeks and banished from the town.

In 1617 a person was pilloried at the Cross and banished for insulting one of the baillies, and in 1640 a female was found guilty of 'unbecoming behaviour' and was sentenced to be scourged at the Cross, drawn in a cart through the streets with a paper crown on her head, a bellman going before her to proclaim her offence, and banished from the town.

Tradesmen who cheated their customers or provided them with shoddy or poor quality goods were put to shame in front of the Cross. In 1787 the magistrates acted against John Collie, a gardener, who was caught giving short measure when selling potatoes. The potato measure which Collie used was said to be 'deficient nearly one-third of the standard', and the magistrates ordered it to 'be broke down at the Cross'.

The Town Drummer attended and proclaimed the name of the owner and user, as well as giving 'the cause of the condemnation'. Then the Common Hangman stepped forward and did his duty. The guilty potato measure was well and truly 'broke'. Justice was not only done, but was seen to be done, for it was reported that 'a great concourse of the inhabitants' turned out to watch the 'execution'.

This kind of public exhibition came unstuck in 1758 when the magistrates decided to burn a book written by Peter Williamson, who as a boy had been kidnapped and sent to the plantations. The book accused a number of prominent Aberdeen citizens of taking part in the kidnapping. The magistrates, declaring that it 'defamed the fair name of the merchants of the burgh', ordered it to be burned at the Cross. 'Indian Peter', as he was called, had the last laugh. He took his case to the Court of Session and won a decree against the magistrates for damages of £100.

There are worse things than burning books and breaking tattie measures. Before the present Market Cross was erected at the end of the seventeenth century, a curious ceremony took place at the old Cross. It was a sequel to the execution of the great Marquis of Montrose at the market cross of Edinburgh in 1650. 'His heid, twa

The Cross as a post office.

leggis and twa airmes were tane frae his body with ane aix, and sent away and affixit at the places appoyntit', it was reported. One of the places 'appoyntit' was Aberdeen.

A dismembered limb from the Marquis's body was exposed on the town's Justice Port and later buried in St Nicholas Churchyard. Some ten years after Montrose's death his son petitioned Aberdeen Town Council to have it restored for decent burial. Although the town had suffered from Montrose, feelings about him had changed; he had come to be regarded as a martyr. The result was that the Council agreed not only to restore the dismembered limb, but to show a measure of atonement.

It was done with great ceremony. Guns were fired from the Market Cross while a procession of town councillors and citizens walked behind a coffin carrying Montrose's limb. They marched from St Nicholas Churchyard to the Town House, where the remains lay in semi-state until arrangements were made to carry them to Edinburgh for interment in Holyrood.

When the Cross was taken down and rebuilt in 1821 the Corinthian column rising from the centre of it fell and broke into three parts. The Cross was black with grime and when it was cleaned up it was found that the unicorn on top of the column was made of pure marble.

In 1842, the Cross was taken down again and moved to its present site at the east end of Castle Street. The masonry filling the arches for the ill-fated Post Office was at last removed and, according to G.M. Fraser, it rose with 'airy gracefulness' and a 'new charm'. It was encircled on its new site with a railing.

'Nowadays', wrote Fraser, 'all classes in Aberdeen look upon the Market Cross as a precious civic possession.' That was a hundred years ago, and it is doubtful if that sentiment still holds good. People have different thoughts on the old Cross. Even in the old days opinions differed – and some people couldn't make up their minds. Walter Thom, who wrote a two-volume history of Aberdeen in 1811, described the Market Cross as 'an erection, neither useful nor ornamental'. That was in the first volume. In the second he praised it as 'a very beautiful and singular production in stone-masonry'. This turn-about came after it was hinted to him that he was on the wrong lines.

Today the ancient Cross, believed to be the finest example of a burgh cross in Scotland, stands a little forlornly in a Castlegate that has long since ceased to be the heart of the city. For years this corner of the town, pulsing with history, rich in the names of famous people, was allowed to become dilapidated and shabby. There have been moves to revitalise it, to rebuild the old houses and lay out a new Plainstones, but the magic has gone.

31

THE RHYMSTERS

Writing rhymes has gone out of fashion. Back in the early days of last century it was all the rage. In 1908, R. Murdoch-Lawrence, who lived in Aberdeen's Bon-Accord Street and was something of a local historian, wrote about the spate of rhymes that had been produced in the 19th and early 20th centuries – children's rhymes, counting-out rhymes, precentor rhymes, and many more.

Murdoch-Lawrence was a member of the Rymour Club in Edinburgh, presumably because Aberdeen had no such club. He had a number of rhymes he wanted to preserve. He laid out a list of them, including many from the North-east of Scotland. One, which came from Catterline and seemed to be tilting at the folk of Johnshaven, was called the 'Haddock and Fluke':

Said the haddock to the fluke
'What mak's your moo crook?'
Says the fluke to the haddock,
'My moo was ne'er even
Sin' I cam' by Johnshaven.'

There was a Buchan farm rhyme in the list. I first heard this rhyme while visiting Pitfour estate, where I was shown the places mentioned in it, and I wrote about it in *Buchan, Land of Plenty*. The rhyme went like this:

At Sapling Brae
I brak' my tae
I shed my horse at Biffie,
I poo'd a wand
On Benwal's yard
An' whuppit on to Bruxie.

Sapling Brae is on the north side of the Ugie Water in Buchan. Biffie and Benwal were adjacent farms on the Pitfour estate (see Chapter 32) and Bruxie Lodge was one of two lodges guarding the estate. Murdoch-Lawrence said that he got the verse from a correspondent whose mother, Isabella Lawrence (1815–1899) was often heard reciting it . Isabella probably came from Buchan.

A signboard outside a hostelry near Tarbet on the west shore of Loch Lomond provided an unusual advertising rhyme. This came from the *Aberdeen Journal* of 8 June 1834, and it invited hungry travellers to come in and eat till they burst:

Mrs M'Phail
Licensed to retail
Spirits, Porter and Ale,
On the afternoon she has for sale
Oatmeal bannocks, Flesh and Kale,
Which travellers hungry and athirst
May swallow till they'd like to burst,
And Mrs M'Phail lets you know
Her charges are all very low.

A rhyme that was popular in Strathdon and Glenbuchat in 1857 told you about the eating habits of the laird of Giltrap:

Sandy Golandy, the laird o' Giltknap
Sup't the brose amd swallow't the caup,
And aifter that he swallowed the speen,
And wasna sairt when a' was deen.

If you weren't fond of brose, and didn't fancy swallowing spoons, there was a rhyme telling you how to prepare a haddock for a meal. It came straight from the haddock's mouth:

The hindmost word the haddock spak'
Was 'Roast my belly before my back.'

Food was the subject of a variety of rhymes. A verse headed 'Tibbie Nicol' was described as 'a domestic inquiry'.

Traycle in a bowie,
Seerup in a cup,
Hey, Tibbie Nicol,
Is yer rhubarb up?

There is nothing to show what sort of dish Tibbie was making with a bowl of treacle, a cup of syrup, and rhubarb.

Then there were puddings – all sorts of puddings. This rhyme was popular about 1840:

White puddings and long,
Blood puddings and short,

Boil'd puddings and raw,
Mingle, mingle, mingled.

Eggs were also on Murdoch-Lawrence's rhyming menu. A verse from Deskry in Strathdon, which was going the rounds in 1870, told of two men who were trying to raise money for tickets to attend a visiting circus – Ord's Circus. They went about selling eggs privately until they raised enough cash for the tickets.

Foggieson and Davidson,
They joined in one accord,
An' sell't their eggs to Jimmy Tam,
An' ran awa' to Ord.

Chapbooks were a source of old rhymes. One called 'Merry Books' came from the Aberdeen University Library at King's College.

Of many books this is the chief,
It is a purging Pill,
To carry off all heavy grief,
And make you laugh your fill.

That was over a hundred years ago, but if anyone wants a good purging it may still be at the University library. Murdoch-Lawrence obligingly left the chapbook's reference number – No. 4.

Just in case you take too lighthearted a view of life, there was also a scarce chapbook, published in Paisley in 1822, which contained a rhyme giving advice on Man's Age. There were twelve different periods or divisions, each with suggestions about such things as 'laying out for a wife', saving something for the children, giving up lust, and preparing for Heaven – 'Lord show thee the way'. The last two lines contained a solemn reminder:

Remember that these divisions post on,
And then this life will quickly be gone.

There were rhymes about the CUCKOO:

In April come he will,
In flow'ry May he sings all day.

About an ITCHY HAND:

Rub it on wood,
It's sure to be good,
Rub it on brass,
It will come to pass.

About SPARING THE ROD:

Spare the rod and spoil the child,
King Solomon said in accents mild,
Be they man or be they maid,
Wollop them well, King Solomon said.

About NOVEMBER'S CHILD:

November's child
Is born to bless,
He's like a song
Of thankfuness.

A nursery rhyme by the Aberdeen poet William Anderson was included in Murdoch-Lawrence's collection. Anderson said it was sung to him by an old aunt. It is more than likely that countless 'wee laddies' were scared out of their wits by it. There were nine verses – this was the fourth:

Has he seen that terrible fellow Montrose,
Wha has iron teeth wi' a nail on his nose,
An' into his wallet wee laddies he throws,
Shoudie, shoudie, pair o' new sheen,
Up the Gallowgate, doun the Green.

These are only a few of the rhymes in the list which Murdoch-Lawrence wanted to preserve, but they give some idea of the wide range he covered in his search. The old rhymes mirrored local history, told us about the day-to-day life of communities, issued weather warnings – 'Cushnie for cauld, Culblean for heat' – gave us riddles to solve, reminded us not to harm spiders – 'If you wish to live and thrive, Let a spider run alive' – and kept us right about the dates of fairs and markets:

Aikey Fair on Aikey Brae,
Is held on the shortest nicht
And the langest day.

When Murdoch-Lawrence wrote about Mrs M'Phail's public-house, with its Spirits, Porter and Ale, he added nostalgically, 'I do not suppose the sign-board is still in existence.' It is more than likely that it was gone then, and it will certainly be gone now. Sadly, the same could be said of many of the places and events depicted in these old rhymes.

32
PITFOUR HOUSE

This magnificent mansion house on the Pitfour estate near Mintlaw once dominated the Buchan landscape. Pitfour House was an architectural curiosity, planned more from a calendar than from a planner's blueprint. It had 365 windows, one for each day of the year, fifty-two rooms for the weeks of the year, and four staircases for the changing seasons. It also had a portico with twelve pillars – one for each month of the year.

The 18th century building was the home of the Ferguson family. The estate, covering 33,000 acres, was bought in 1700 by James Ferguson, an advocate at the Scottish bar. He was the first of six Ferguson lairds who lived there in the two centuries that followed.

They lived in great style, gaining a reputation for lavish spending and eccentricity. They laid out a huge lake, built stables and lodges, scattered rococo statues about the estate, laid out a racecourse (today you can walk round it), built an Observatory (now in the care of the district council and open to the public), and dug out a canal from Pitfour to the sea.

Pitfour House.

When I was shown round the estate a few years ago, it had shrunk to less than 500 acres. I passed an open piece of ground which had been allowed to grow wild as a haven for birds. This was where the mansion house had been, but there was nothing to show that it had ever existed.

The house with 365 windows and fifty-two rooms was demolished in 1927, the year that the picture on the previous page was taken.

33
HATTER TO THE PEOPLE

The ghost of Samuel Martin will tip his hat to you if you pass the site of his old shop in Union Street. Keep an eye open and you might see him standing in the front of what was originally No. 34 (now Esslemont and McIntosh), wearing a red Garibaldi shirt, a brown velveteen coat, a waistcoat – and a fancy head-dress. He was, after all, Hatter to the People.

Sammy was ahead of his time. Born in Hamilton, he came to Aberdeen in 1837 and opened a hatter's shop in Union Street in 1838. He met fierce competition, but he countered it with a publicity and advertising campaign that would have been more in tune with the new millennium than the 1840s. His shrieking headlines told the world that the Hatter to the People had arrived.

Canny Aberdonians shook their heads and said it would never last . . . he was wasting his money . . . he was more like the *Mad Hatter* than a responsible businessman. But his hat news leapt from the pages of the *Aberdeen Herald* – Satin hats, amazingly attractive; Felt hats, New Shapes, Intellect Improvers; Summer Caps, some cool, all comfortable – and people started flocking to his shop.

Sammy was a man with views on everything from the nasty Russians and the Crimean War to the fate of the Working Classes and the activities of the Queen Victoria and 'her happy Family', and he used his advertising space in the *Herald* to air them. When the queen arrived at Aberdeen on her way to Balmoral, the headlines in his advertisement read:

Three Cheers for our Noble Queen. HURRA! HURRA! HURRA!

While proclaiming loyalty to the Crown, Sammy didn't forget his hat business. 'Being of opinion that a proper attention to Dress should be studied by all her Majesty's subjects, particularly on an occasion of this kind,' he wrote, 'and as the HAT is the most conspicuous part of man's dress, Martin would respectfully suggest to the Public the propriety of appearing before her Majesty with a *Good Hat*.'

He wanted to avoid 'what might be an unseemly sight to Royalty – viz., to be received by the Waving of Thousands of Old Hats'. This

Samuel Martin.

could be avoided by buying one of Martin's beautiful satin hats, with nice showy linings, pleasing to the eye.

It was said that the *Aberdeen Herald* wouldn't have been a paper at all without Martin's advertising. Sammy never missed putting an 'ad' in it, but there was a suspicion that he himself never wrote the material. It was thought that it was done by a little man called Kelman, but no one really knew. William Carnie, who worked as a reporter on the *Herald*, told what happened when the employees were taken on their annual outing to Huntly. In the Square, Carnie saw the local barber, Rob Smith, standing at the door of his shop along with 'a boorichie of critics and other shavers anxiously taking stock of the *Herald's* leading lights'.

'Having known Rob in his Aberdeen apprentice days,' Carnie wrote in his *Reporting Reminiscences*, 'I advanced to greet him for auld lang syne. After a few casual remarks – "Man," quoth Rob, "we were jist trying to pick you fellows out, and guessin' which wiz the real clever chaps. Aye, wiz we, and we wid like fine to ken fitch o' ye writes the advertisements o' Sammy Martin, the People's Hatter!"'

Sammy was as proud as a peacock when he was told about the conversation in Huntly.

The Hatter to the People continued his weekly commentaries. In 1856 the so-called Arrow War broke out in China when the Chinese captured a lorcha, or junk, flying the British ensign.

INSULT TO THE BRITISH FLAG AT CANTON

thundered the Herald headline. Here was 'work for China menders', said Sammy, demanding the 'Immediate Chastisement of Britain's Enemies'.

He told his readers that British factories had been destroyed by the Chinese, but he had no idea that one of them – a shipbuilding business at Whampoa near Canton – was owned by an Aberdeen man, William Couper, who was later kidnapped by the Chinese. He was never seen again. Even without that terrible news, Sammy called on Britain to pitch into the Chinese in true British style. 'Would-be poisoners and treacherous foes deserve no quarter,' he declared.

Sammy must have been proud of the role he played in the building of one of Queen Victoria's statues in Aberdeen. When the idea was mooted early in 1864 he wrote a McGonagall-style poem backing the proposal and suggesting a suitable site:

> St Nicholas Street corner really would be
> A very nice site, 'The People' may see,
> Couldn't be better, tho' they give a small bounty,
> And would likely be pleasing to the Town and County.
>
> And tho' not made of Granite there's no need to garble
> T'will look very well of Sicilian Marble.
> The Queen, God bless her, is a nice canty bodie,
> And that Statue may please if done by A. Brodie.

The statue, which was unveiled by the Prince of Wales on September 20, 1866 was the work of local sculptor Alexander Brodie; it was made of Sicilian marble, and it stood on a site at the corner of St Nicholas Street and Union Street. The self-styled Invincible Hatter had triumphed again.

Another statue – the Duke of Gordon's statue in Castle Street – also caught his attention on two occasions. The first was in October, 1857, when two Russian guns taken at Sebastopol during the Crimean War were placed on each side of the Duke's statue. Sammy thought that this was 'the most proper (and conspicuous) place in Aberdeen'. An alternative site must have been considered, for he added scathingly,

'The idea of placing them permanently in a Cabbage Garden of an Hospital may well appear to many more farcical than logical.'

The Duke of Gordon came into his sights a second time in January, 1874, when it was planned to put a horse trough beside his statue in Castle Street.

A HORSE TROUGH UNDER A DUKE'S NOSE

said the headline in the Herald.

WHAT NEXT!

Below was another piece of Martin doggerel:

Methought I heard the Stone Duke say
Oh! pray take this vile trough away,
Councillors might very well suppose
'Twould spoil my view and offend my nose.
Truly, if I could get away,
I would no longer near it stay;
'Tis most unseemly to the eye –
Remove it quickly let 'The People' cry.
Oh! 'Twould surely be a pity
To insult my memory in the Granite City.

Crimea, China, trouble at home, mutiny in India (he called the mutineers 'beasts in human form') – the Hatter to the People was always ready to offer advice. 'If the Queen (Long Life to her Majesty) commands Martin to appear at Balmoral to hear his opinion upon the Indian crisis, or other matters', he wrote, 'Martin would humbly lay before her Majesty a few reasons and suggestions'.

He wondered if the Queen might see her way to making him a knight or a peer ('Lord Martin would sound well enough'), but it never happened, and it is highly unlikely that he ever really thought it would. It never affected his loyalty. His cup overflowed when the Queen and the Prince Consort paid a ceremonial visit to Aberdeen on 15 October, 1857.

The route of the royal procession passed No. 34 Union Street. The *Aberdeen Herald* reported that 'our trusty friend, Mr Samuel Martin', was at his upper window 'energetically sending forth from a French horn or cornopeon the well known notes of 'God Save the Queen'. On ceremonial occasions he was often seen 'blowing loyal tunes out of a bugle'.

When the procession was over Sammy held 'open table', making all and sundry welcome to cake and wine. The *Herald* said that it

GLORIOUS RESULTS OF DECISION!

END OF THE PERSIAN WAR!

PRELIMINARIES FOR A NEW PEACE.

LATEST NEWS FROM CANTON!

WAR going on, daring attempt to destroy the British Fleet with fire Ships nobly frustrated by Britain's blue jackets being on the alert. But all the British factories (with very few exceptions) destroyed by fire by the Chinese, who in their incendiary warfare, imagine they are exterminating what they call the barbarians, by destroying their property. Meanwhile, Admiral Seymour gallantly keeping his position, intrenching himself in the Factory Gardens preparatory to destroying Canton, which appears to be the only way to bring the Chinese delusionists to their senses. Meantime, unexpected

DEFEAT OF THE BRITISH MINISTRY,

for countenancing the acts and nobly taking the responsibilities of their representatives at Canton, in gallantly chastising the Chinese for insulting the British flag; for, although there is evidently a diversity of opinion in high quarters, as to the intent and extent of the insult, yet that the flag was insulted there can hardly be a doubt, and MARTIN THE HATTER's idea is, that whenever and wherever the British flag is insulted, the only answer should be

Prepare for Action and Fire away!

Thus MARTIN was well pleased with the decision that Admiral Seymour displayed. But it is a melancholy and disastrous fact that there is a strong tendency in Britain of late years to find fault with her Diplomatists and Naval and Military Commanders —melancholy, when not always just, and disastrous from the consequences it may lead to. There are no class of British subjects who have the honour, dignity, and welfare of their country, more at heart than Diplomatists and Naval and Military Commanders, and it is in accordance with common-sense, that, were it not so, they could never have obtained the confidence of their Government or the positions they severally hold; and when such men are placed in positions with power to act according to their discretion in matters affecting the honour and dignity of their country, and when having done so to the best of their abilities, 'tis as unseemly as it appears unjust to hear faults found with their conduct by parties at home, who possibly mean well for their country, but would do well to be perfectly satisfied of their competency to judge before giving a deprecatory opinion of brave men, who are hourly chancing their life's blood for the honour of their country, and whose greatest ambition may be to serve their country well and merit the thanks of their Government. But when such men hear of severe comments approaching to censure upon their conduct where they may have expected praise, 'tis enough to make brave men shrink from the responsibilities of active service, seeing their country apparently so reluctant to encourage merit, or to appreciate brave deeds. So thinks

SAMUEL MARTIN,
HATTER TO THE PEOPLE,
34, UNION STREET, ABERDEEN.

Established Nineteen Years.

MARTIN'S Stock is very large at present. Beautiful SATIN HATS, New Shapes, easy-fitting, light, and durable, 6s. 6d., 8s. 6d., 10s. 6d., 12s. 6d., 13s. 6d., and 15s. 6d. ; best quality, 18s.

One of the advertisements by Sam Martin, the Hatter to the People.

had its own notion of the music, but the wine was good and the decoration of Mr M's establishment was unmatched in the city.

On 17 October his advertisement in the *Herald* carried the heading:

> WELL DONE, ABERDEEN! Splendid, magnificent, gorgeous, pleasing, gratifying, thrilling, transcendently perfect . . .

He finally ran out of adjectives to describe the occasion. 'Aberdonians, generations to come will read with glowing admiration your doings on the 15th October, 1857, he wrote.

Samuel Martin, Hatter to the People, was a publicist beyond compare. He was controversial. He was funny. He was over the top. But he was also a superb salesman, never forgetting that he was a Hatter – *the* Hatter, for nobody could match him in Aberdeen. His motto for Martin's hats was simple:

> LOOK WELL, WEAR WELL FIT WELL, and PLEASE WELL.

Martin died in January 1888. He was buried in Nellfield Cemetery and the inscription on his stone, read, 'The Last Resting Place of Samuel Martin, Hatter to the People, Aberdeen'. In his *Reporting Reminiscences,* William Carnie recalled how he had discussed Sammy's death with the well-known journalist and author, William Alexander. They felt it was a distinct loss to the town, for he had brought a bit of colour to local everyday doings.

'The mere mention of his name', wrote Cairnie, 'brings vividly before the mind's eye the smart, dapper, jaunty figure, morning after morning for a long series of years, briskly holding on his way to the well-frequented No. 34 Union Street.' He had heard the name 'mountebank' used about him, but Samuel Martin was a gentleman – an eccentric gentleman – with a clear head and a kind heart.

'Possibly the pervading ambition of Mr Martin's life was to be spoken about at Balmoral during the visits of our beloved Queen to Deeside. For many summers and autumns he regularly resided at Ballater near the foot of Craigendarroch Hill, and as he was ever on the best of terms with John Brown, Her Majesty's favourite personal attendant, there existed pretty good reason to believe that the name of the "Practical Hatter" with the knightly aspirations was not quite unknown within the Royal family circle.'

Sammy would have liked that.

34
WALLACE AND THE TOWER

I'm the auldest man that's ever lived
in Aiberdeen,
Oh, lots an' lots o' famous things an'
people I hae seen,
I can min' when Wallace in this city
spent an 'oor,
I went an' hid a drink wi' him inside
the Wallace Tower.

Harry Gordon sung that song, 'The Auldest Aiberdonian', in his Invernecky days at Aberdeen. Harry, or his song-writer, Archie Hyslop, turned history on its head for the sake of a laugh – it was one of the local stories that 'professors didna ken'. But the real link between Scotland's national hero and the Wallace Tower has come under more serious scrutiny over the years.

For a long time it was thought that the effigy of a knight in armour in a recess in the tower *was* William Wallace, but there has been no shortage of people lining up to scoff at the story. In 'The Auldest Aiberdonian' there is a line saying, 'list to local stories G.M. Fraser disna ken'. Fraser, who was Aberdeen's librarian and a well-known historian, did 'ken' about the Wallace Tower story.

In his *Aberdeen Street Names*, he rejected the Wallace theory, but accepted that the origin of the legend may have lain with the knight holding a sword. The Tower originally stood by the Netherkirkgate and Carnegie's Brae. Fraser thought that the figure was put up about the middle of the 18th century by John Niven, a tobacco and snuff manufacturer. He said it might have been taken from nearby St Nicholas Churchyard, leaving the uneasy impression that it had been nicked. This thought may have been nurtured by the fact that in the old days such memorial stones were 'looked upon as so much rubbish'. Even so, most people would have taken the stolen effigy story with a pinch of salt – or snuff.

Just to confuse the issue, old pictures of the statue show the sword in different positions. In one, it is held upwards, while in another it is downwards with its point resting on the ground. This is supposed

The old well at Carnegie Brae, with the Wallace Tower behind it.

to have happened when 'Wallace' was repaired and given a new arm. The sword was described by a workman as 'sheet-iron turned in at the edges', and 'clorts o' paint'. He was even less impressed by the statue itself. 'The hale rickmatick' [the whole lot], he said, 'is so frail-like that I'm fley't [scared] to lay a han' on't'.

So the mystery of the Wallace Neuk and its Tower lingers on. How *did* it get its name? An alternative suggestion was that it took its name from a well that stood at the top of Carnegie Brae. Old prints, in fact, show two different types of street well at the Neuk. In one, a woman and child are seen drawing water from an ordinary well. The other shows a busy scene at a large four-sided stone well with a pyramid-shaped upper half. A horse and cart are seen struggling up the Carnegie Brae filled with barrels of water from the well.

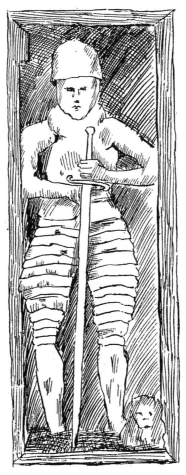

Wallace and the Tower. This old sketch shows the Knight with his sword pointing downwards.

It is this picture that makes you wonder if G.M. Fraser was wrong and if, after all, this was the origin of the name – the Wellhouse Tower and not the Wallace Tower. Fraser, however, wouldn't listen to any other theories. 'We must just continue to work with the Wallace tradition,' he wrote, 'amused a little at the quaint and unwordly figure which has presented itself to passing generations of Aberdonians as an embodiment of the Champion of Scotland.'

In 1964, in the face of strong opposition, the Wallace Tower, which was one of only four remaining 16th-century buildings in Aberdeen, was demolished to make way for a store. It was rebuilt, using some of the old stonework, on the Motte of Trillydrone near Seaton Park. The purists regarded this as a pseudo-towerhouse and the pseudo William Wallace perched in his niche in the wall virtually moved out of the public eye.

35
GHOSTLY GATEPOSTS

Up on a windy hill near Oyne you look across the Garioch to the gurgling waters of the Gadie burn and beyond it to the seven peaks of Bennachie. This is a land of myth and legend, a land cluttered with old Pictish symbols and heavy with the memory of Dunideer and its 'thirty thousand Heilanmen' marching to Harlaw. It is peppered with Recumbent Stones and Upper Pillars. It was once said that in the huge masses of the Oxen Craig and the Mither Tap, standing stones 'piled up upon one another like gigantic books'.

There is a stone circle on the whin-covered hilltop at Hatton of Ardoyne. The name Ardoyne means 'high Oyne' and the true dialectal sound is Ardeen. The change from the original Een to

The stone circle at Hatton of Ardoyne, with Bennachie in the background.

Oyne was partly blamed on the coming of the railway. When an engine puffed into Oyne in the railway's early days the porter would cry, 'Een! Een!' and often a mocking voice would reply, 'Twa, man! Twa!'

The farm of Hatton of Ardoyne stands on a side-road going north to Old Rayne. A rough, rutted track runs up past the farmhouse to the stone circle. Most of the stones are scattered and broken, but the recumbent stone, one tall flanker and three more stones are still standing, plus the remains of the inner ringcairn.

The circle is well-known , but its popularity is enhanced by the strange, mystifying story attached to the stones. People come from far and near to see the place where a farmer stirred up unseen forces when he disturbed the stones at Hatton of Ardoyne. He wanted them to make gateposts for one of his fields, but when the gate was built he couldn't get his horses through them. Nothing would make them pass between the two stones.

Eventually, he decided to put the stones back in the circle and all was well. But then there was another disturbing development. It had taken the strength of two horses to drag each stone down the hill, but it required only one horse to drag one stone *up* the hill. That was two centuries ago and no one has ever come up with an explanation of how it had happened.

There are always people tramping up that muddy track to see the stone circle – and maybe to come up with their own theories. Not long before I was there a team from Cambridge University had been studying them, and some time before that a man from Warwick University had come to inspect them. He thought it had something to do with magnetism in the stones.

I stopped at the farm to chat to the farmer, Harvey Jaffrey, and his wife Elsie. Harvey had been in the Merchant Navy, but took over the farm when his father died. He thought that the strange goings-on had taken place in 1790, but he could shed no light on it. I asked him if he knew who the farmer had been at the time and the reply surprised me.

'It was my great-great-grandfather,' he said. 'His name was Alexander Jaffrey.'

I asked Harvey if he believed the story about his great-great-grandfather and the stones that frightened his horses.

'No!' he replied emphatically.

Most people would dismiss any suggestion of other-worldly

Harvey Jaffrey on his farm at Hatton of Ardoyne, with Bennachie in the background.

interference, but it takes on a different complexion when you learn that there were similar occurences at other stone circles in the North-east. One was at the Mains of Hatton at Auchterless. What happened there was a complete duplicate of the events at Hatton of Ardoyne – the two stones, the gateposts, the fearful horses, and so on.

The Auchterless stone circle was mentioned in an article written by James Ritchie in 1926 for the *Proceedings of the Society of Antiquaries*. Part of it dealt with 'the influence of Good and Evil Spirits'. Ritchie said that the idea that stone circles and standing stones were under the special care of the spirit world was widely prevalent at that time.

'Many years ago,' he wrote, 'some of the stones of Mains of Hatton Circle, Auchterless, were removed to form gateposts, but the spirits, it is said, resented human interference with the circle, and it was only with great trouble that horses could ever be induced to pass through the gate. So little was the farmer prepared to encounter the spiritual enmity this clearly indicated, that he decided to replace on their original site the stones which had been taken away; but it was remarked that while two horses with difficulty dragged each stone downhill to the gate, only one found it easy work to pull a stone uphill from the gate to the circle.'

Ritchie said that a somewhwat similar story was told of the Drumel Stone on the farm of Old Noth, near Gartly. The stone was taken to the farm to make a lintel over a doorway in the steading, but after that the door was frequently found open and the animals out and wandering about the countryside. It was decided to put the stone back again and when this was done the trouble ended.

The farmer at Auchleven, Premnay, was less lucky. He removed *all* the stones from a local circle and shortly afterwards many of his cattle died from disease. He seemed to get little comfort from his neighbours. They regarded the fate of Auchleven as a judgement on him for destroying the circle. A farmer at Cairnfauld in Durris also lost his cattle herd by disease after he had removed stones from a nearby circle.

So could there really be some link with the spirit-world, or was it just another fanciful tale that had come drifting down the years, like all the other curious tales about stone circles? Another story is told of a cairn near Cairnie called the Monk's Cairn. It marks the spot where Thomas Gordon of Ruthven killed a monk from Kinloss and it became the custom to add a stone to the cairn when you passed it. If you didn't do that it was considered unlucky.

Then there was the Killishmont cup-marked stone at Keith. This stone on the Helliman Rigg had nine cup-marks in three rows. When a tenant tried to cultivate the area near it one of his oxen fell dead.

There is a final twist to the tale of the standing stones. James Ritchie said that the spirit influence didn't always *protect* ancient monuments; it was sometimes antagonistic to their preservation. This was shown at a stone circle with the odd name of Chapel o' Sink, south-west of Inverurie. Long, long ago an attempt was made to build a chapel within the stone circle, but each night the walls sank out of sight. The building always started again in the morning. The work eventually had to be abandoned.

36
SOAPY OGSTON

When an Aberdeen business man, Alexander Milne Ogston, built a mansion-house on Lower Deeside in 1878 he modelled it on the Scottish baronial style of Balmoral Castle. Now, well over a hundred years later, it is a well-known up-market hotel, but it has retained its original name – Ardoe House. Inside the hotel there is an Ogston suite with a dining capacity of 200, more for conferences. There is also a family room with a name that puzzles many guests – Soapies.

To the business community, Alexander Ogston was one of the city's leading lights – a soap manufacturer whose name was known not only to generations of Aberdonians, but, as the *Aberdeen Daily Journal* once put it, to 'every household in the country'. To ordinary Aberdonians, however, he was simply 'Soapie' Ogston, whose factory dominated the area between Loch Street and the Gallowgate. His grandfather started the business in the late 18th century and 'Soapy' joined the company as a teenager in 1855.

The Ogston empire had its roots in Loch Street. In the 1820s it had a candlemaker's business at 52 Loch Street, and after operating as a tallow chandler, became a soap and candlemaker at 84 Loch Street in the 1850s. It amalgamated with the Glasgow firm of Charles Tennant in 1898, when the company's office was switched to 111 Gallowgate.

Soapy Ogston's works covered several acres of a great square bounded on the west by Loch Street, on the north by Innes Street, on the east by the Gallowgate and on the south by McKay's Close. Innes Street is still there, but McKay's Close, which ran from the Gallowgate to Loch Street, has vanished. It was known locally as Candle Close, a name kept alive by the Candle Close Gallery at 123 Gallowgate. There is also a Candlemakers Lane.

It was in this huge area of the old Lochlands that the factory had its soap-making and candlemaking departments, its margarine department, its refinery for refining paraffin wax, its box-making department and its cooperage. This was where they built up a world-wide reputation for candles of all description – and for 'hard, soft, toilet and powdered soaps'.

The entrance to Soapy Ogston's in the Gallowgate.

The Northern Co-operative Society – the 'Co-opy' – was a near-neighbour of Ogstons and I remember talking to Dick Simpson, the society's publicity supervisor until his retirement, about the old days at Soapy's. Dick's father was distantly related to the Ogstons (his name was Edwin Ogston Thomson Birnie Simpson), but the nearest Dick came to an association with the King of Soap was when he worked as a boy with the Co-op and handled the goods from Ogston's factory. The bars, he said, were about 15 inches long – great cakes of plain, yellow soap.

'Soapy's' connection with the business spanned ninety years, covering a period when great developments took place. It was said that Alexander and his younger brother, Colonel James Ogston of Kildrummy, made the name of Ogston and Sons 'a household word at home and of wide repute abroad'. In 1905, however, disaster struck – the factory was devastated by the worst fire the city had ever seen.

It all began when someone on the second floor of a house at the foot of Innes Street looked out of a kitchen window and saw a light flicker in a bottom window of the candle store directly opposite. Within minutes the inside of the building was completely illuminated. It was the start of a blaze that was to end in big headlines splashed across the pages of the *Daily Journal*:

GREAT FIRE IN ABERDEEN
ANOTHER OUTBREAK AT OGSTON AND TENNANTS
CANDLE-MOULDING DEPARTMENT DESTROYED
EXCITING SCENES – FIREMEN INJURED.

The first fire had been on 13 August the previous year. It had broken out in the same place, the paraffin wax store, although in a different part of the building. The store in 1905 contained about 150 tons of paraffin wax in barrels, 60 tons of tallow, about 50 tons of caustic soda and potash, and a quantity of resin. As the *Journal* commented, 'It can readily be imagined with what terrific fierceness such inflammable materials blazed.'

Just how bad it was could be seen from the reaction of the public. 'Many people', reported the *Journal*, 'seemed to think that the city had been suddenly overwhelmed by fire, and for a time there was an extraordinary panic.' The paper carried a graphic description of the fire. The smoke was so thick that people couldn't see each other a yard apart. Women shrieked in terror as they ran to get out of it. Mothers screamed for their children – 'My God! Faur's my bairns?'

'Huge volumes of dense, suffocating smoke belched from the burning building and the scene in Innes Street and the Gallowgate was for a time almost indescribable,' said the *Journal*. Householders in the few houses on the north side of Innes Street were driven into the street by the smoke. 'For a time it was feared that not only the great works in which it originated, but large stretches of property in the thickly-populated surrounding locality would fall a prey to the devastating flames.'

The fire raged with 'terrific fury' in the refinery; it had the appearance, it was said, of a huge glowing furnace. Flames licked at hundreds of barrels of paraffin wax and finally burst from every window. One mighty crash was heard, then another, as the thick concrete floors dividing the different storeys fell in huge slabs. The burning roof crashed in and a pillar of flame shot high in the air.

The fire could be seen all over the city and thousands of people flocked to Loch Street to watch the blaze. The south end of the Gallowgate was crowded with sightseers, held back by the police. Barrels of fat burst, setting off explosions 'like a big battery of artillery'. Gallons of water and paraffin wax melted by the fire flowed down the street, at times nearly a foot deep. Dean of Guild Alexander Lyon and two newpapermen saw a tiny rivulet suddenly turn into a fiery torrent which cut off their retreat. They were faced with the prospect of having to wade knee-deep across a lava-like stream, but escaped by grabbing some empty boxes and planks and using them as stepping stones.

Melted wax formed a small sea which cooled and set into a hard mass, but immense quantities of it flowed down the sewers, raising fears that it would harden and choke the pipes. Every man that could be spared was hauled in and given pails and scoops, any sort of container they could lay their hands on, to catch the escaping fluid and pour it into empty barrels.

Alexander Ogston, told of the fire by telephone, raced into Aberdeen from Ardoe to direct operations for salvaging stock and checking the flames. A huge pile of company books was taken from the office to the stables on the west side of Loch Street. A detachment of Gordon Highlanders arrived from their depot to assist the firemen.

'The building was now practically in ruins,' the *Journal* reported, 'but the blaze mounted high in the air and roared with fearful splendour, while the lurid glare and the dense, impenetrable smoke rolling across the heavens presented a spectacle of awesome grandeur. Still the men worked bravely on, and returned to the attack again and again. The boxmaking factory was completely at the mercy of the flames. The inflammable fuel burned with extraordinary fierceness and the interior of the building, as the flames hissed and roared, presented a fearsome spectacle.'

Sailors from a Navy vessel called the *Cockatrice* arrived to help out, cheered on by the spectators. 'Working like Trojans', they used special tackle to pull down walls that were in a perilous condition. Men from the Cleansing Department were put to work scraping and breaking up greasy matter which had poured from the works in streams. As it cooled it 'caked' and made walking dangerous.

Meanwhile, plans were being made to house people who had been made homeless by the destruction of three tenements in the Gallowgate and Innes Street. Some had lost everything except the clothes they wore.

The Mission Hall of the Gallowgate U.F. Church was gutted – 'a victim to the devouring tongues of flame whose progress nothing could check'. The roof of a nearby public house became 'a living mass of fire' and it, too, was gutted. The margarine department next to the refinery was burned to the ground. More barrels of fat burst, the glowing ends of the casks shooting high in the air and 'resembling for the moment a balloon'.

By eight o'clock in the evening the excitement in Loch Street had died down – the fire was well in check. Great crowds of people thronged the streets until late at night, kept at a safe distance by the police. When it was all over, Alexander Ogston was able to give an assurance that the manufacturing parts of the works – the soapmaking and candlemaking departments – had escaped the fire. The workers jobs were safe. 'Soapy' Ogston was back in business.

Ogston and Tennants' were taken over by Unilever after the last war. Today, the only reminder of the great soapworks that dominated the Gallowgate and Loch Street is a granite-fronted office at No. 111 Gallowgate, which has the name 'Ogston and Tennant' above the door. Out at Ardoe, where Alexander Ogston had the reputation of being a good laird, people wine and dine in the house that he built for his wife. They sit in front of a roaring fire in the Laird's Bar, or they take a snack in a family room with a name that was once a household word at home and abroad – 'Soapies'.

37
THE NAKED REGIMENT

It was a day that was long remembered by the people of Aberdeen . . . the day that a regiment of soldiers dropped their trousers in one of the city's main streets.

The scandal never found its way into the history books, but in 1795 it set the whole town talking, brought the wrath of the City Fathers down on the head of a notable street character called Alexander Ross, and ended up in a 'burning' on the city's Plainstones.

Sandy Ross, *alias* Saunders Ross, *alias* Statio Ross, *alias* the Flying Stationer, was a kind of cultured jack-of-all-trades. He wrote and sold broadsheets and published a 'History of Aberdeen', which he sold in penny numbers, but he also mended china and dazzled his public with a peep-show in the Castlegate.

He was well-known in Aberdeen at the end of the 18th and the beginning of the 19th century. He kept the public well-informed on what was happening in the world, circulating all the latest news and gossip to citizens taking their daily stroll on the Plainstones. Tall and thin, his faced pitted with smallpox, he was regarded as a wit and a satirist. 'The man must have had a heart of lead and a timmer-cap kind of skull who would not have winced under the sarcastic lash of old Saunders Ross,' wrote William Bannerman, who featured him in his book, *Aberdeen Worthies.*

On Friday mornings he would appear with a small trestle under his arm and carrying a show-box on his back. This was the man-size equivalent of the cardboard peep-shows with which Aberdeen youngsters amused themselves before the last war. Statio used drawings, slides and wax figures; one of his scenes had a waxwork shoemaker 'working away as if the Devil himself had been in him'. This frenzied activity came from a string which Statio pulled at the back of the box.

He had twelve subjects in his box, ranging from 'The Taking of Quebec in North America' and 'The Wandering Jew of Jerusalem' to 'The Whole Royal Family of Great Britain, in figures of Real Waxwork'.

The Flying Stationer kept up a steady commentary during his

performance. He had a nice line in patter for his 'Very Grand View' of St Peter's Church at Rome – 'The Pope says the gates of hell cannot prevail against that church, neither shake it nor tremble it, but faith, if it be upon my back on a windy day it shakes me most damnably.'

Enter Colonel Leith. He was the Colonel Blimp of his day, who had his own private army, a regiment of volunteers whose fitness for soldiering was often in doubt. It was said that when he recruited men he 'gave eyes to the blind and ears to the deaf', and that he made the deformed walk straight. Once they were enlisted, he provided them with regimental dress.

The day came when the Colonel took stock of his regiment and decided to get rid of the dross. They were classified as 'inefficients'. 'A great many were put aside by the General as unfit for service,' it was reported. There was nothing private about the disbanding. It took place in Castle Street, where people were going about their business. Before the rejected volunteers were sent on their way, however, the Colonel decided that they should return their uniforms, which he regarded as his own private property.

So there, under the astonished gaze of passers-by, the men were ordered to drop their trousers. They were 'stripped unceremoniously', according to William Bannerman. 'This was done in so unseemly a manner that the kind-hearted females of the east end of the town were under the necessity of lending them clothes, for decency's sake.'

The townsfolk were outraged. There was such a hue and cry against the Colonel that Sandy Ross decided that it would make a suitable subject for his show-box. As William Bannerman put it, 'The Stationer considered this a fit subject to appear upon the stage *sans pareil.*' He called it 'Leith's naked regiment' and turned all his wit and sarcasm on the man who had brought it about.

The Colonel was not amused. He complained to the magistrates that he had been insulted. The result was that 'Sanney' was sent to prison for one month and his show-box was ordered to be burned at the market place at the hands of the common excutioner. The Stationer watched from a window in the 'Burgher's room' as the flames licked up over the box and, as Bannerman reported, 'in one ignominious pile fell the great St Peter's of Rome and the whole Royal Family of Great Britain'.

When 'Sanney' got out of prison he had no money, no box and no future, so he decided to call on the citizens of Aberdeen for help. He wrote a poetical address with the title: 'Poor Sanney's

The Castlegate - scene of the Naked Soldiers affair.

Tragical, Comical, Farcical and Whimsical Address to his old and best friends, the Public.' He asked them to 'raise a poor but honest fallen neighbour out of misfortune's ditch' and went on to tell 'the melancholy story of my Box':

> A Tale – enough to soften even rocks,
> While I in view confined – (in durance vile)
> Stood and beheld the dismal sight the while.
> Had I been seated on the Weather-Cock,
> Instead of being under key and lock,
> Regardless of the awful giddy height,
> My Box to 've rescued, I had ta'en my flight,
> And o'er the heads and backs – (nor think I joke)
> Had bent a hazel stick – or knotted oak.

He went on to say that winter had spread its chilly carpet over the land and he needed their help:

> Some timely aid, my Friends, or Sanny's gone,
> My limbs are motionless, my blood is froze,
> The icicles are hanging to my nose –
> O Sirs, be quick, I'm standing at Death's door –
> Help, or your Flying Stationer's no more.

Beef and coal were expensive – 'and Whisky, too, the comfort of the Soul', and all he wanted was twopence, or even sixpence, to buy a crust of bread and cheese. He also had to pay Burnett and Rettie, a Netherkirkgate firm of printers and publishers, for printing the Address.

Sanney ended his Address like this:

> Be not too sparing of this World's vile dross
> But throw some pence to
> Yours
> Poor Sanney Ross.

Nobody could ignore such a cry for help. Poor Sanney got the support of his public and with the profits from his broadsheet was able to make a new show-box and new subjects.

Bannerman recalled seeing him many years later. 'It was evident from the stoop in his gait, the support he needed from his stick, his sallow complexion and strong hectic cough, that he had nearly "strutted his hour", and that the curtain would soon drop upon old Saunders Ross,' he wrote.

Alexander Ross was a cut above the other cranks and pedlars who frequented the Castlegate two centuries ago. 'There was no individual in any grade, in his own time, living in Aberdeen, that could bear a comparison with him,' wrote William Bannerman. 'However humble his various vocations were, in the exercise of them he never forgot the dignity he owed to himself – as a worthy, decent citizen'.

The broadsheet which Sanney sold to re-establish himself became very scarce. A correspondent writing to *Aberdeen Journal Notes and Queries* in 1911 said he had only seen one copy of it. 'It is a real local curiosity,' he declared.

38
BENDELOW'S PIES

They would stand in Aberdeen's Causewayend and sniff the air like the original Bisto kids. It sometimes seemed as if half the town had been drawn to the street by the aroma – the smell of Bendelow's pies. It was summed up in a verse written by Lord Provost George Stephen, the city's postie-poet, who wrote couthy poems about the city:

> First in priority, better than a'
> Nae matter the shape or the size,
> Was the scrumptious aroma they smelt far awa,
> The smell o' John Bendelow's pies.

The pies were made in a little shop in Causewayend (they called it Cassie-end), next to the school. In those halcyon days between the wars, the school's hungry pupils would descend on the pie shop like vultures during their break. The girls' playground formed the boundary between the shop and the school and youngsters bought their pies and bannocks through a window in a back wall of the shop.

The scrumptious aroma that people 'smelt far awa'' wasn't the only odour that wafted over to Cassie-end. People who lived there can still remember the less scrumptious smells that floated over from the Broadford works, the jute factory in Froghall and the Aberdeen combworks. That was in the days when the combworks turned out 9 million combs annually. It was said that if they were laid side to side lengthways they would extend to about 700 miles.

George Stephen's poem told about the factory girls who came down to Causewayend on pay night to buy Bendelow's pies. This is what he wrote:

> When weemin were vrochtin the roon o the clock
> At the Jute Works or Broadford's auld mills
> They'd set aff wi' a shawl and a kwite owre their frock
> To try to get owre a' their ills
>
> By gaun ilka pay-nicht along Cassey-eyn
> To buy there o' mair than ae size

Sae tasty as kitchie, het sappy and fine,
Jist ane o' John Bendelow's pies

Some nichts for variety, eence in a file
A fine fatty bannock they'd buy,
And gulpin' it doon in the open air style
'Twas nearly as gweed as a pie.

When my wife, Sheila, was growing up in Elmbank Road she often crossed the Tarry Briggie on her way to Causewayend, taking a look over the brig at Izzy Masson's farm before making her way to No. 42 to get pies for her family. 'It was a real treat!' she remembers, whether it was mince pies *or* apple bannocks. The shop had a sign above the door, 'R. Jessamine', for it was the Jessamine family who sold the Bendelow pies and bannocks that teased the tastebuds of Aberdeen folk.

The founder of the firm was said to be Jane Bendelow, daughter of John Bendelow, a hotel waiter. The Bendelow family tree shows that John Bendelow (1841–1908) and Mary Ann Edward (1837–1901) were married on 22 November, 1862. They had three daughters: Elizabeth, Susannah and Jane. Jane (1866–1938) married Robert Simpson Jessamine in 1892.

Although Jane appears to have been the driving force behind the great Pie project, her father must have been heavily involved in it, for people always spoke about 'one of John Bendelow's pies'. Garth Jessamine, great-grandson of the Bendelows, thought that the family came from Cracow in Poland and that the name was originally Bendelowski.

Robert Simpson Jessamine was the first to carry on the Causewayend business, followed by his oldest son, Robert Bendelow Jessamine, who was born in 1893. This was the family that made Bendelow's pies legendary, not only in the Mounthooly area, but throughout Aberdeen, and even well beyond it.

I was given some idea of how far their reputation had spread when Garth told me how he once gave his name to a new security guard in London and was asked: 'Fit wye are ye nae up in Aiberdeen makin' pies?'

There were people and places in Cassie-end whose names have become part of the Cassie-end folklore. The painter Alberto Morocco went to Causewayend School. His father sold ice-cream from a barrow before buying a shop opposite the school. Jeannie

This picture of the Jessamine family shows R.S. Jessamine in the centre of the front row with his wife Jane (Jane Bendelow) on his right. Note Jane's skirt – the photographer painted in an extra six inches of her skirt because her husband thought it showed an indiscreet amount of leg. Their sons and daughters are as follows: Back, from left, Edith, R.B. Jessamine, Hilda, Austin and Alice. Seated (left) is Edmund and on the right Elizabeth and J.E.B. Jessamine. Picture courtesy of Garth Jessamine.

Robertson, the well-known folk-singer, lived at No 45 Causewayend. The 'Bobbies' Boxie', a police sub-station, was a familiar landmark and next to it was a tenement, Nos. 6–10, owned by Walter Michie. He had his grocer's shop on the ground floor. I knew Walter and golfed with him many times before his untimely death.

Cassie-enders got their pies from Bendelows, but their intellectual sustenance came from a 'fleapit' in Nelson Street called the Globe Cinema, better known to its patrons as the Globey. There were 'penny matinees' on Wednesdays and Saturdays and it was said that if you went in wearing a shirt you came out with a 'jumper'.

The jokes flew thick and fast about the Globey, but Bendelows was also a target for wisecracks. When they showed silent 'flicks' at the Globey, someone stood at the back of the screen providing the dialogue. During one scene, when a posh lady was entering her carriage, the voice behind the screen gave an order to the coachman: 'James, drive me down to Bendelows.' That got a roar of applause from the audience.

'Who's got eyes like Bendelow's pies?' was a well-known chant. Garth Jessamine's cousin, John (his father, Edmund Jessamine, was a dentist in Belmont Road) told me that in his time in the late 1940s and '50s they had three pie sizes – a ha'penny pie, a tuppeny pie and a thrupenny pie. 'One hole, two holes and three holes,' said John. Big apple pies were called Bannocks – Fatty Bannocks. The Fatty Bannock was a monster, about 1 ft in diameter. 'I tried to eat one once and was flummoxed,' recalled John, who now lives in Leamington Spa. "You could get eight portions out of it.'

Bendelows was a very small shop. It had one of the old brick and stone fireplaces – and the fire was never allowed to go out. It was attended to on 365 days of the year. The shop didn't open on Christmas Day, but the fire had to keep burning.

John remembers that they had to stand on a table when they handed out pies through a window to the Causewayend pupils. When they were running out of pies they cut them in half and sold them for a penny.

The Jessamines lived at No. 48 Elmbank Terrace. Garth Jessamine recalls that Saturday lunch for the girls working at the Causewayend shop was prepared at No. 48 and his job as a youngster was to carry it down to the shop on his bicycle with the heavy containers hanging from his handlebars. On one occasion he came to grief. When the shop girls ate their lunch they didn't know that some of the potatoes they were eating had been rescued from traffic on the Tarry Briggie.

The coming of the Roundabout saw the end of Bendelows. Robert Jessamine's shop, along with the properties of Joseph Carcone, Walter Michie and Forbes Wright, had all been acquired by the Aberdeen Council by 1962 in preparation for the develoment of the area. Cassie-end became a dual carriageway in 1972 and a new two-and-a-half acre roundabout – some folk called it Aberdeen's Piccadilly Circus – mushroomed at the end of it.

Now, nothing remains to remind us of the time when, as George Stephen said in his poem, women from the Jute Works or Broadford's mills would leave their work on pay-night and set off to get hot, sappy meat pies from Bendelows. This weekly ritual was recalled in a letter written by a Mrs Pat Lattimore, Banchory:

'Round about the turn of the century,' she wrote, 'when working hours were from 6 a.m. till 6 p.m. the women workers at Broadford Mills, the Comb Works and the Jute Works in Aberdeen had an invariable custom on Thursday evenings of queuing for the purchase of pies at John Bendelow's Pie Shop.'

Long after Bendelow's pies were just a fragrant memory, letters to the local papers stirred memories of the Great Pie days. Among a number sent to me by John Jessamine was one from a Mrs J. McHattie, Seamount Court, Aberdeen, who had been a pupil at Causewayend School. This was what she wrote:

Bendelow's was in Causewayend, right next to Causewayend School, which I went to 50 years ago. I remember they had a window overlooking the playground, where one pane of glass was removed and we could shove in our hand, with a halfpenny in it, and we got a great big pie, twice the size of the ones you get today, and full of mince. A' for a maik! But please, the apple tarts were never called that, they were big bannocks – fatty bannocks. Oh, for one of them now!

When the bulldozers descended on Cassie-end and Mounthooly thirty or forty years ago they demolished more than Bendelow's Pie Shop and the Bobbies Boxie – they wiped out a whole way of life. The last word came in a poem by Elizabeth Keith. Its title was 'Cry for a Pie' and it was published in the *Press and Journal*'s North-east Muse. This was what it said:

Ye dinna need yer specs tae see
Things are'na what they used to be,
Folk canna sing withoot a mike,
Revered professions go on strike,
Aul' standards in their tatters lie
And what has happened to the Pie?

A memory to all held dear
The glorious pie of yesteryear
The pastry melted in yer moo'
And inside lurked the savoury stew –
Protein enough to feed the Navy,
Chunks o' good beef and loads o' gravy.

Now reared on such nutricious food
Our local lads abroad made good
Dining at eastern banquets nightly
Wielding their chopsticks most politely

Ye'd hear an ambassadorial sigh –
'I wish I hid a Jessiman's pie.'

Shame on this thin resistant crust
(To draw comparison we must),
On contents of the brittle shell
We likewise sound a doleful knell.
Oh! greeny-grey amorphous mass
Is this for beef supposed to pass?

Ye Bakers at your early shifts,
Directors in your dizzy hichts,
Ye Butchers buyin' at the mart,
Heed our poor muse and mak' a start:
Though ither schemes gang far agley
Muster your guns and save the pie.

But nothing could save the Great Pie – not even the Directors
in their dizzy hichts. Maybe it is just as well, for where in this day
and age could anyone get a monster pie for a mere half-penny – a
humble maik!

39
A DOOK IN THE BATHS

A young couple laze in the sun on a grassy mound above the promenade at Aberdeen Beach, unaware that they are sitting on a piece of local history.

Buried beneath the mound is the rubble of the old Beach Baths, where for over seventy years generations of Aberdonians learned to swim. When it was demolished in 1972 the city engineer, William Turner, said that the site should be laid out as a focal point. He put forward one idea that he thought would be appropriate – a sitting area.

If the Baths had been in better shape in its later years (it was said to be rusty, smelly and in a dangerous condition), an imaginative town council might have retained it as a holiday attraction – a vivid landmark, a red-brick Victorian folly that would have outdone in colour and bad taste the 'little Blackpool' that has sprung up along the sea front in recent years.

The building, designed by city architect John Rust, was opened in 1895. Whatever today's seaside revellers might have thought about it, it was regarded at the time as a tremendous asset to the city. It consisted of two sections, a new main block with a swimming pool and, linked to it on the north side, a 'baths station' for private baths.

One report on the building drew attention to the two square towers in front of the bath house. These, flanked by a turret at the new south wing and an ornamental chimney-stalk 70 feet high, presented 'a neat and compact appearance, the compressed Ruabon brick imparting a warm dash of colour in pleasing contrast to the green sweep of links amid gleaming sands and the blue expanse of sea'.

The swimming pool in the new south wing was 90 feet in length, 35 feet in breadth, and was 'situated in an underground building'. The pond was 'surrounded by forty-five dressing boxes, and all round is a gallery, capable of accommodating 1,200 spectators'. The baths station section on the north side of the complex had 'wings containing the ladies' and gentlemen's baths – plunge, spray and shower baths in the first-class rooms, the same minus the shower in the second-class rooms'.

Bathing Station, Aberdeen Beach. Aberdeen artist, Jimmy Sutherland's painting of the Beach Baths.

But Aberdeen's ornate pavilion of red Welsh brick was not the city's first bathing station. Back in the summer of 1867 the following advertisement appeared in the *Aberdeen Journal*:

> The Bathing Establishment on Sea Beach
> is now in full operation.
> A bus leaves West End of Union Place every lawful
> day for the Beach, at Seven o'clock Morning, and
> Eleven o'clock Forenoon.
>   Aberdeen, 19th June, 1867.

This was the original hot sea water baths, housed in a building which looked like a row of cottar houses. A tall chimney rose up at one end, forerunner of the lofty 'chimney-stalk' on John Rust's baths. A photograph taken in March 1868 shows benches and forms in front of the building, while women attendants in aprons stand on the veranda awaiting their clients. Curiously, a donkey and a pony, presumably there to give rides on the sand to the bathers, can also be seen on the veranda.

These old hot-water baths were gone by the turn of the century, replaced by Rust's building. But the north section of the complex, incorporating a shelter and tea room, eventually became shabby

Sitting on a memory . . . the old Beach Baths were buried under this grassy mound.

and dilapidated and was demolished. Today, people who went to the Beach Baths in the period up to its closure remember only the building with the swimming pool, where sea smells and the hot breath of chlorine drifted up as you went underground to have a 'dook', undressing in one of the 'dressing boxes'.

A kiosk at the entrance sold pails and spades for making sand castles on the beach and outside the building was a First World War shell used as a collecting box for charities. Ten swimming clubs used the beach pond and it was there that prominent swimmers like Dolly Murray, Irene Barrie, the Fordyce brothers and many others did their training.

The halcyon days of the Bathing Station at the turn of the century are recalled in a painting by Aberdeen artist Jimmy Sutherland. There it is in all its red-brick glory, smoking pouring from its 'chimney-stalk'. Ladies with parasols walk on the 'prom', while down below a scattering of women and children stroll or sit on the sands. But there are no bikinis here, only long black dresses and straw hats. A bathing coach stands ready for anyone bold enough to take a dip.

The painting is from an old photograph taken by James Porter, a photographer for the *Aberdeen Free Press and Evening Gazette*. Born in 1874, he also had a photographic business in the city and took pictures of the royal family at Balmoral. He died in 1938. His daughter, Mrs Gertie Still, who has books of his photographs, remembers the old Beach Baths for another reason – she went there to swim every Sunday morning when she was a young girl. That was in the days when Andy Robb was coaching up-and-coming swimmers at the 'downtown Baths'.

The Beach has recently undergone radical change, not to everyone's liking, but back at the end of last century they were no less ambitious. Plans were made to build a marine aquarium in the old bathing station, and when that didn't come off they talked about opening it up as a grotto. To the north of the station there were to be 'swing horses, trapeze, parallel bars and other gymnastic apparatus'.

Today, all those dreams and others that followed are buried under the grassy mound on the edge of the promenade. Like that young couple taking the sun, you can sit there and sniff the sea breezes . . . and maybe a whiff of chlorine will come drifting up out of the past.

40
COCKY HUNTER

It was once said that the name of Cocky Hunter would always have a place in Aberdeen's history. That thought was reinforced a few years ago when a new bar was opened in Union Street – it was called Cocky Hunter's Bar!

The entrance to it was decorated with the kind of bric-a-brac that might have graced the Hunter store in Castle terrace in the old days . . . a wash-house mangle, a kist, a souter's last, a few dusty old literary tomes with names like *Bible Cyclopedia* and *The Humanitarian*.

The Bar didn't last long, but every time I passed it I thought of the piece of doggerel that was chanted by youngsters in Aberdeen in the years before the war.

> If ye want a knocker for yer door,
> Or a hoose tae fit yer floor,
> Ging tae Cocky Hunter's store
> In Aiberdeen.

There were actually three Cocky Hunters in Aberdeen over the years. Their reign spanned two world wars and stretched over seventy years. The nickname 'Cocky' was handed down from father to son like a title, and if there had been a family coat-of-arms it would probably have shown a needle and an anchor, with a market cross representing the Castlegate. Their motto would have been 'We buy or sell anything'. The Hunters had their roots in the second-hand furniture trade. Members of the family branched out on their own, but they mostly followed the same line of business and all stayed within reach of what became their spiritual home – the Castlegate.

The first Cocky was Thomas Hunter, whose smart, dapper appearance won him the nickname that was to become a byword in Aberdeen. Postcards in Hunter's Bar in Union Street show a bowler-hatted 'Cocky' with a bushy moustache, wearing a white shirt and tie, and sporting an Albert across his waistcoat. He was born in 1867 in Water Lane, off Virginia Street, only a short distance from the streets where the Hunter 'dynasty' founded its 'needle to an anchor'

The first 'Cocky' Hunter and the interior of Cocky Hunter's Bar.

empire. His birthplace lay below Castlehill, where another 'Cocky' Hunter was to carry on the family tradition.

Young Thomas Hunter left school at the age of thirteen and had his first taste of trading when he took a job with a fish dealer. He was given a pony and two-wheeled cart and sent off to the fishing villages south of Aberdeen to buy speldings. He worked as a boiler-maker in shipyards in Aberdeen and West Hartlepool before returning north with a wife who was to bear him sixteen children. In 1903 he opened his first second-hand furniture store in East North Street, followed by another in Commerce Street.

When there was a market in the Castlegate he would get up at four o'clock in the morning, load a handcart with goods, and push it up the hill to his stance. He always said that he could supply his customers with anything they wanted, but some people set out to prove that it was an idle boast.

One man walked into his store and asked for a half loaf. It so happened that Cocky had bought a loaf for his morning piece and had only eaten half of it. The customer walked out with the other half – and a lost bet. Another trickster asked for half a pound of dulse, but Cocky's luck held. By coincidence, a fisher wife called Old Betsy, who wandered around the city with a creel of buckies and dulse, called at Cocky's shop. Another bet was lost.

While Cocky's business developed, his sons and daughters branched out on their own. Alec had a cycle and accessory business in Exchequer Row, on what is now the site of a supermarket. Albert had a furniture and tools business, and Josephine, the eldest daughter, had a similar shop in Castle Street. Lily, another daughter, followed Alec's example and opened up a cycle and pram depot and Rita was also in the furniture trade in the Gallowgate and George Street. Maude, the youngest, opened a ladies' and children's outfitters in Queen Street and Castle Street.

When Cocky died in 1925 at the early age of fifty-eight he had become a legend. At his funeral, it seemed as if the whole city had turned out to pay their respects. Everyone from civic dignitaries to the humblest of Cocky's customers was there, packing the streets so tightly that it took the cortège four hours to get from Commerce Street to Trinity Cemetery. His coffin was carried by boiler-makers.

Cocky's youngest son, Bill, recalling the funeral many years later, said that when walking in the procession he had to keep his head down because the sea of faces was so overpowering. The gates of Trinity Cemetery were kept open until eight o'clock at night so that people could file past his grave.

It was the end of an era, but the name Cocky Hunter was to remain a byword in the city. The mantle fell on his eldest son, Alec, who in 1932 moved from his business in Exchequer Row to open up a second-hand store in South Mount Street. Here, and in the Castle Terrace store in later years, Cocky Hunter's business literally reached bursting point.

The South Mount Street building covered nearly three acres of ground and was bounded by South Mount Street, Richmond Street and Kintore Place. I was brought up in the Rosemount district of the city and often passed Cocky Hunter's on my way into town. Or didn't pass it. More often than not I was drawn into it to gaze in awe at the chaotic wonderland inside . . . it was a magical place for a youngster. Bedsteads, bikes, wireless sets, doors, tools, barrows, desks, prams; there was everything except the kitchen sink, and *it* was probably hidden away somewhere in that three-storey house of wonders.

There were probably coffins there, too, for Cocky bought a number of coffins from the ARP just after the last war. They say that a joiner bought some on condition that nobody told his wife, who was a regular customer, where the wood had come from. The deal was struck and for all we know the joiner's wife is still blissfully sleeping in a bedroom furnished with a suite made from Cocky's coffins.

Alex Hunter often told the story of a glass hearse he bought in Oldmeldrum. When he was there he also bought a grandfather clock, which was slipped into the hearse where the coffin normally lay. At Oldmachar a policeman saw the 'coffin' in the hearse, held up some schoolchildren, and gave a smart salute as the hearse passed by. The same thing happened again at Split the Win' in Aberdeen.

Cocky was a bit of a practical joker. An old friend walked into his store looking a little the worse for drink and Cocky made out a placard, 'Kick Me Hard', and stuck it on his back. He had a box in his store which had a note on top of it saying 'Please don't open this box'. Cocky would hide himself and watch customers carefully lifting the lid and gasping with horror, for inside the box was a skeleton.

What I remember most about the South Mount Street store was how half its contents seemed to spill onto the pavement. Sideboards, tricycles, old paintings, rolls of linoleum, seats . . . they piled up until pedestrians had to sidestep to get past them. The same thing happened when Cocky Hunter moved to Castle Terrace – bikes, beds, chairs and tables overflowed on to the pavement. It could never happen today.

The move to Castle Terrace came after the South Mount Street store and all its contents were destroyed by fire in 1937. It was a return to the Hunter heartland. Alec took over the old Sick Children's Hospital in Castle Terrace and it remained as Cocky Hunter's until 1972, although Alec died in 1961. His only son Tom took over the business.

Although Cocky No. 2 was the King of Junk, his taste rose above the bric-a-brac in his store, for he was an expert on such things as antique furniture and porcelain. He was basically a shy person. The aristocracy was among his customers and he was often invited to dine in the stately mansions of the North-east. He always declined; he believed that everyone had his place, and his was not at the tables of the gentry. He refused social invitations and never wore 'tails'.

Left: Cocky Hunter's Bar in Union Street. Right: It might be a corner of Cocky's old store . . . it is, in fact, a corner of the entrance of Cocky Hunter's Bar in Union Street.

One of his customers was Lady Burnett of Leys, who often asked Cocky to buy antiques for Crathes Castle. Shortly after the Castle Terrace premises opened she saw a fireplace in the building and asked Cocky if he knew that it was an Adam. 'Fine that!' said Cocky. When asked what he was going to do with it he replied, 'I'm takkin' it oot. Wid ye like it?' Lady Burnett was delighted and when it was installed she invited him to Crathes Castle to see it. He never went.

Aberdeen's couthy Lord Provost Sir Thomas Mitchell, one of Cocky's close friends, was a regular visitor to the Hunters' home in Castle Street, but when Tommy invited them to his farewell dinner he turned down the invitation. He felt it would be out of place to dine with the city's upper-crust.

Alec's brother, Bill, Thomas Hunter's youngest son, who took over the Commerce Street shop in 1940, was also known as Cocky. When plans were being drawn up in the early 1970s for a new inner ring road from Virginia Street along Commerce Street to East North

Cocky Hunter's premises in Castle Terrace, with goods spilling out on to the street.

Street, it looked as if Cocky's of Commerce Street had come to the end of its days. Given notice to quit, Bill started to sell off his stock. The ring road plan was held up and he started to buy in stock again, but in January 1972 he was given just over a month to get out.

At that time, looking back over his Commerce Street years, he had regrets at the way he disposed of some of his goods. 'My father always said to keep a thing for seven years,' he said, 'but I can remember tearing up brass candlesticks for scrap at twopence a pound'. Time was also running out for the last bastion of the Cocky Hunter empire, the Castle Street store. When Alec's son, Tom, took over the store after his father's death he got rid of much of the stock and concentrated on furniture. In 1973, however, he was approached by a southern firm who wanted to buy the store and demolish it to make way for a new development.

Tom decided to sell after seeing a plan of the Castlegate of the future. It showed trees growing on Castle Terrace – and no sign of Cocky Hunter's. There are now trees in the Castlegate, which has been pedestrianised, but no trees in Castle Terrace. Instead, a huge new housing complex has been built on the site of Cocky Hunter's store, stretching all the way down to Virginia Street.

It was once said that the name Cocky Hunter would always have a place in Aberdeen's history. Whatever the future holds, if you go down to the Castlegate, listen hard enough, and let your imagination stretch a little, you might still hear an echo of that old familiar chant floating up over the hill: 'If you want a knocker for yer door, or a hoose tae fit yer floor . . .'

41
THE COLLECTOR

When George ('Taffy') Davidson was a small boy he would lie awake at night listening to the rattle of a 15th-century claidheam mor (broadsword) that hung on the wall of his bedroom. His father was an antique collector, and another article that fascinated the lad was a snuff-mill that was cleaned once a year so that the inscription on it could be read. Then, at the age of six, young George bought the first item in his own collection – a snake in a jar.

In years to come, Taffy Davidson's interest in antiques was to put him in the front rank of antique collectors, propel him into a curator's post with Aberdeen University, and lead to a curatorship with the Highland Folk Museum at Kingussie. He could have had a career in art, or in the building and slating business inherited from his father, but it was said that 'he became side-tracked by antiques and their time-consuming acquisition'.

This magpie of the antique world left Aberdeen Grammar School in 1911 to study painting at Gray's School of Art. The award of a post-diploma year in painting took him to the Continent. In August 1914, when the Germans invaded Belgium, he was in the Netherlands. He made his way home, catching the last trawler to leave the Low Countries for Britain, and when he arrived in Scotland he enlisted as a private in the 4th Battalion Gordon Highlanders.

Asked what his job was, he said: 'An artist'. He was sent to paint the latrines. Despite this humbling start to his war service he was in action at the Ypres salient, suffering gas attacks and bombardment. Half a century later he was reminded of the battle while working at the Highland Folk Museum in Kingussie. On 18 July 1968, he wrote:

> It's 53 years today since I saw the Chateau de Hooge blown up and lost my bootlaces running over the ridge doing messenger boy to our bombers. So a bus of les Belgiques had to turn up (at the Museum), steal flowers and refuse to pay their shillings. I still had a few appropriate words to address them with. They used to take the handles off their wells when they saw the kilt! We did not like les Belgiques. Ni moi trop plus?

In France he drew and sketched portraits of his comrades in the trenches. He even found time to add to his collection. One war 'souvenir' he picked up was a piece of stained glass from the shattered cathedral of Ypres. In September 1915 he was badly wounded at the Menin Road and sent home. He was demobilised in December 1918 and returned to Art School in Aberdeen to resume his post-diploma course.

When his father died he took over the family business, but continued painting and collecting. Every Friday he could be found at the stalls in the Castlegate market, rummaging among the bric-a-brac for hidden treasures. He arrived and departed in style – by taxi. His reputation grew and he was appointed part-time Curator of Paintings, Silver, etc. to Aberdeen University. In 1954 he gave up the family business to become curator of the Highland Folk Museum.

Titles meant little to Taffy. He regarded professional curatorship with a slightly jaundiced eye, as he did the views of so-called 'scholars'. 'Revive the old Scottish antiquary and his fireside collection,' he wrote in May, 1959, 'else the wiseacres – so scientific about it all – will scare any audience ower the hills and far away.' Taffy certainly didn't scare them ower the hills; in his first ten years at Kingussie the number of visitors increased and several thousand objects were acquired for the museum.

'We are a little up on last year and mostly satisfied customers,' he wrote in June, 1969. 'The gardener in absentia I got a tip of four bob (my record). I hand these on to him. Mrs D. is very despondent about tips. She's never got one. She attributes my success to my slovenly appearance. Of course, I do take my hat off!'

Taffy's notes and letters and other papers relating to his work are now in the Marischal Museum, where the bulk of his collection is housed. They shed some interesting light on both Taffy the Man and Taffy the Collector. He had no time for 'modern art', and while helping to chose sculptures for an exhibition, said that he ought to resign because he was always saying 'No'.

When one particular work was being considered it got a mixed reception. Someone finally said: 'It might look well in a stony background.' 'Yes,' said Taffy. 'I know the very place – the bottom of Rubislaw Quarry.'

He mixed with the high and the humble – and learned from them. For example, an old man he met at the side of a ditch in Perthshire showed him – 'as a favour' – how to make money from dirt. 'He selected a flawed brown pearl,' wrote Taffy, 'rubbed damp earth on his hand, then worked his two palms like he was "murling doon" his tobacco. He then showed me a marvel, a perfect pearl of pale pink.

Taffy Davidson.

He'd skinned it. It had not the brilliance of another, but he explained that some jewellers didn't know. He bought his raw material from the boys until they found him out.'

In 1962, Taffy drew up 'A Description of the Things in Room I' of the Folk Museum. Among them was a 'horn spoon mould belonging to Kyard Young celebrated in several 'Leaps' on our burns'. This was Jock Young, a member of a notorious family of 'cyards' (tinkers) who gave his name to 'Jock Young's Loup' near Potarch Bridge on Deeside. According to Davidson, he was caught near Banff about 1800 and convicted of a murder in an old barn.

He also had a letter box which John Brown put before Queen Victoria every morning at Balmoral. 'This box I bought from a sale at the house of John Brown's nephew about thirty years ago,' he wrote in 1974. The box, he said, was 'tinker-made, probably from crown pieces', and after Prince Albert died a tinker inlaid the border of the lid with a nielo band made from lead and sulphur.

Taffy had a great affinity with tinker folk. They scoured the countryside in search of material for him and his museum at Kingussie. Jock Mearns, a collector himself, knew Taffy better than most people. They met when Taffy bought some sketches from him, and their mutual interest in collecting led to a friendship that lasted until Taffy's death.

Jock's interest in antiques dates from his wartime days in the Army, when he took two small Capo-di-Monte figures home from Italy. 'I was helluva hard up', he recalls, 'and I sold them. The chap who bought them offered me so much that I thought, "Why does he see something in them that I can't see?" That was the start.'

In the basement of his house in King Street Jock has a workshop packed with collectors' items ... everything from a painting of Findlater V.C. to an old clock and medals given to a nurse in the first world war – and a painting by Taffy. Along the corridor is a wine cellar, chock-a-block, not with bottles, but with paintings, sketches and prints. Jock showed me a long sword which Taffy had given him. The date on it was 1680.

Down in that dingy basement we sat and talked about Jock's friend and mentor. When he went to Kingussie he told Jock that if he ever saw anything worthwhile he had to buy it and take it up to him. He had his own way of putting his seal of approval on a purchase. 'If a thing wasn't right,' said Jock, 'he would say, "That's nae the mealy tattie." If it *was* right he would say, "That's yer mealy tattie".' Jock took up a small Scots bairn's chair he had bought in Ellon. It passed the mealy tattie test. 'It had to be right,' said Jock. 'That was the main thing. Monetary value was not in it.'

But Taffy could be moody. 'You could never approach him about buying anything from him,' said Jock. 'He didn't like that.' He was, however, always a generous man. When he died in October, 1976, Professor R.D. Lockhart wrote a tribute which described his fresh complexion, with never a wrinkle, and the twinkle in his eye; the sombre tweed suit he wore, with a generous expanse of waistcoat – and always the most expensive grey homburg hat in a large size.

'He belonged to this North-east land,' said the Professor. In other words, Taffy Davidson, the man who was 'side-tracked by antiques', the man to whom collecting became an obsession, was always the real mealy tattie.

42
DOWNIE'S CAIRN

Half-hidden behind bushes at the junction of Tillydrone Road and Tillydrone Avenue is a 9-foot-high red granite obelisk – a monument, according to a partly-obscured inscription at the bottom the the cairn, to George Downie or Dauney, a sacrist at Aberdeen University in the 18th century.

It marks what became known as Downie's Slaughter, a curious tale that first appeared in print in 1825. Downie was a sacrist who was the terror of the students, always ready to 'lift up both his voice and cudgel' against erring students. They plotted their revenge. One day, twenty of them grabbed him and hauled him off to a room laid out as a court of justice. Downie or Dauney was arraigned, tried and found guilty of tyranny in his office. He was sentenced to be beheaded.

They blindfolded him, led him to another room, bound his hands behind his back and then removed the bandage from his eyes. Horror-struck, the Sacrist saw that the walls of the room were hung with black. In the middle of the room stood a huge block and nearby a brawny student holding a great axe. Another student held a towel. Behind the block was a basket of sawdust and a tub of water.

Downie threatened his captors, then pleaded with them to end what he thought was a jest. A student with a towel began to scatter sawdust round the block – and the sacrist became convinced that his time had come. He dropped to his knees, admitted his faults, and asked them to release him. He was laid on the block and his face was covered. The student with the towel dipped it in the tub of cold water, swung it back like an axe, and brought it down on Downie's neck. He gave a groan and died.

Downie was found lying cold and stiff in the middle of the library, dead from heart failure. The key of the room was in his own pocket. All the paraphernalia for the gruesome hoax had vanished – and the students with it. The identity of the guilty men remained a secret, although fingers were pointed at a student called Robert Mudie, who first told the tale of Downie's slaughter in 1825. Born in Monymusk, he was the son of a sexton and beadle there and his grandfather was a sacrist at King's College.

Downie's Cairn.

Today, a question of another kind remains unanswered. There is no trace of a sacrist called George Downie in the records. The cairn at Tillydrone Road was moved to its present site in 1926 from a landscape garden at Berryden, and one theory is that it was simply a folly.

The final piece of the jigsaw is a piece of low ground at Berryden, near Back Hilton Road. It was known as Downie's Howe, and it was traditionally believed to have been the sacrist's burial place. Here, another doubt creeps in. The actual name of the howe is not unlike the name Downie – it comes from the Gaelic *dunan*, meaning a hillock. So, putting all the pieces together, did the mock trial of George Downie ever take place? Or was the tale of Downie's slaughter itself a hoax?

43
THE HAPPY JAILBIRD

Prison escapes, rooftop protests, riots . . . it sometimes seems as if the inmates of our jails will do anything to get out of their cells. But not always. Take the case of Robert Smith, a farm worker, who appeared before Lord M'Laren at the Aberdeeen Circuit Court on 1 July, 1893.

Smith was found guilty of culpable homicide, causing the death of a fellow workman and fatally injuring another man on a farm near Stonehaven. The case was described by Lord M'Laren as being on the very edge of murder. Sentenced to penal servitude for life, he vanished behind the grim walls of Peterhead Prison.

After he had served part of his sentence, his old employer went to see him at Peterhead. He mentioned to him that a petition might be raised in an effort to have him released, or at least to have his sentence shortened.

Smith was horrified. 'Dae nae such thing,' he declared. 'I was niver sae comfortable and happy a' my life. The meat is guid and aye sure, and ye ha'e a roof abeen yer heid. It's far better than hyowin' neeps an' howkin' tatties.'

As far as is known, the happy jailbird served out his sentence without any other attempts to put him back into the cruel world outside Peterhead Prison.